The Tea Lover's
DEVOTIONAL

Emilie Barnes

HARVEST HOUSE PUBLISHERS

EUGENE, OREGON

Unless otherwise indicated, all Scripture quotations are taken from the New American Standard Bible®, © 1960, 1962, 1963, 1968, 1971, 1972, 1973, 1975, 1977, 1995 by The Lockman Foundation. Used by permission. (www.Lockman.org)

Verses marked NIV are taken from the HOLY BIBLE, NEW INTERNATIONAL VERSION®. NIV®. Copyright © 1973, 1978, 1984 by the International Bible Society. Used by permission of Zondervan. All rights reserved.

Verses marked KJV are taken from the King James Version of the Bible.

Verses marked NLT are taken from the *Holy Bible,* New Living Translation, copyright © 1996, 2004. Used by permission of Tyndale House Publishers, Inc., Wheaton, IL 60189 USA. All rights reserved.

Verses marked TLB are taken from *The Living Bible,* Copyright © 1971. Used by permission of Tyndale House Publishers, Inc., Wheaton, IL 60189 USA. All rights reserved.

Cover by Garborg Design Works, Savage, Minnesota

Cover illustration © Camille Ellerbrook / Indigo Gate, Inc.

Harvest House Publishers has made every effort to trace the ownership of all poems and quotes. In the event of a question arising from the use of a poem or quote, we regret any error made and will be pleased to make the necessary correction in future editions of this book.

THE TEA LOVER'S DEVOTIONAL

Select devotions and content are taken from the following: *Meet Me Where I Am, Lord; Minute Meditations™ on Prayer; The Twelve Teas® of Inspiration; If Teacups Could Talk*

Copyright © 2009 by Emilie Barnes

Published by Harvest House Publishers Eugene, Oregon 97402

www.harvesthousepublishers.com

ISBN 978–0-7369–2235–7

All rights reserved. No part of this publication may be reproduced, stored in a retrieval system, or transmitted in any form or by any means—electronic, mechanical, digital, photocopy, recording, or any other—except for brief quotations in printed reviews, without the prior permission of the publisher.

Printed in China

15 16 17 / RDS-SK / 10 9 8 7

To all the women who love to have tea
with both strangers and friends...

I encourage each of you to add
one more element to your habit of tea—
that of enriching your life
with healthy reading materials.

*Whatever is true, whatever is honorable,
whatever is right, whatever is pure, whatever
is lovely, whatever is of good repute, if
there is any excellence and if anything
worth of praise, dwell on these things.*

PHILIPPIANS 4:8

These pages will be an encouragement to
your heart and soul as you take time to sip
a cup of hot tea. May your life be blessed
as you experience tea and good reading!

Tea and Devotions

*Nature meant very kindly…when she made the
tea plant; and with a little thought, what series
of pictures and groups the fancy may conjure
up and assemble round the teapot and cup.*

WILLIAM MAKEPEACE THACKERAY

The ritual and nature of tea invites us to pause during our day and to indulge in a soothing ritual. We put the kettle on the stove and decide which kind of tea suits us. Then, we select a favorite cup. Whether it is fragile and elegant or sturdy and practical, once our cup is filled, we get to take in those first breaths of tea's rich aroma. We're lucky if our day's schedule allows for time to sit and savor, but even if we have only a few minutes, tea makes those few minutes rich and enriching.

Some of us remember sitting down to tea with our mothers, grandmothers, or special mentors, and those memories flood us with the warmth of closeness and connection. The simplicity and comfort of tea gives us this same sense of connection with God. When we slow down, we have time to express our gratitude, lift up our needs, and seek God's heart. And when we share tea with others, we can extend our understanding of faith to them, heart to heart.

These devotions and the accompanying tea-related recipes and sidebars are a perfect match. When we take the time for simple pleasures, like the ritual of tea, we also calm our thoughts and worries, and we make room for the ritual of spending time with God. Whether your heart is fragile or strong right now, when it is filled with the wisdom and grace of God, you can take in faith's rich aroma. It will sustain you and inspire you.

Let's fill our cups together.

Emilie Barnes

The Name of God

To Seth, to him also a son was born; and
he called his name Enosh. Then men began
to call upon the name of the LORD.

—GENESIS 4:26

Throughout the book of Genesis, God uses different names for Himself to reveal certain aspects of His character. These names are especially important to a people with no written record of God's words and deeds. The character of God becomes clearer as He reveals His names, including...

- El or Elohim—which means His strength and power
- Jehovah—which means "the self-existent One," I Am who I Am
- Jehovah-Jireh—The Lord will provide
- Jehovah-Rapha—The Lord who heals
- Jehovah-Nissi—The Lord our Banner
- Jehovah-Shalom—The Lord our Peace
- Jehovah-Raah—The Lord our Shepherd

- Jehovah-Tsidkenu—The Lord our Righteousness
- Jehovah-Shammah—The Lord is present

These names of God reveal who He is—His character, His nature, His being, His attributes. When we enter into prayer, there is no way we can approach God as the "Big Daddy" or "The Man Upstairs." Our knees should tremble when we are in God's presence. We want the whole world to know what a privilege it is to go into prayer with God, whose name is above all names. He is great; He is mighty; He is majestic!

The way God has made Himself known to others enriches the depth and richness of our worship today. When we better understand the nature of God through His various names and what they mean, we can begin to grasp the vastness of who God is and who He is in our lives.

❖ PRAYER ❖

Father God, as I look upon Your majesty through Your various names, I begin to grasp Your awesomeness. My limited mind prevents me from realizing how big You are. You are certainly an awe-inspiring God. I praise Your name always. Amen.

❊ HEART ACTION ❊

Spend time with the Lord so that you truly know Him and His nature. Invite Him into your home daily so that your family and guests all can learn more about Him.

The true gift of a teatime celebration...fills our cups with joy and warmth. May the echo of the teacups' message be heard not only on special occasions, but anytime friends come together.

EMILIE BARNES

Happy Husband's Help

*All of you be harmonious, sympathetic,
brotherly, kindhearted, and humble in spirit...
You were called for the very purpose
that you might inherit a blessing.*

—1 Peter 3:8-9

A number of years ago Bob and I were in Charleston, South Carolina, touring an old African-American craft district, when we ran across an apron that had "If Mama Ain't Happy, Nobody's Happy" embroidered on it. We realized that the maker of this apron had captured the essence of marriage. In a healthy marriage both partners are happy in the roles they play. When a spouse is happy and feels appreciated, he or she will want to be of help to the other. If your mate is unhappy, the last thing he wants to do is help you out or please you.

I certainly recognize and acknowledge that you are not responsible for your husband's happiness; he alone must be accountable for that. However, we as wives do play a large part in making our mates feel appreciated. Don't take it for granted that he is thoroughly aware he is appreciated. As a marriage partner, it's important that you take the time to show and say verbally that your mate is appreciated for all he does for the family. In most cases his boss at work gives him little praise for his efforts, so your family's praises might be the only positive affirmations he receives each day. As marriage partners, we want to treat our spouses as well as we treat our close friends.

Bob and I genuinely want to share our appreciation for each other. We never want to take anything for granted. We often say, "Just another way to show that I love you," before we do a courteous act to or for each other. A little "thank you" goes a long way to show our mates that their acts of efforts are appreciated. Make today a new beginning of loving and caring and serving in your marriage.

❋ PRAYER ❋

Father God, from the bottom of my heart I want my husband to know he is appreciated and loved. I want to show him how much I like the things he does for me and our family. Let today be a new day in our lives. May I be willing to treat him like a king, so he can treat me like a queen. Amen.

❋ HEART ACTION ❋

Give thanks for the blessings in your life. Celebrate them and share them. It is easy to be gracious when you live in God's grace.

Bread and water can so easily be toast and tea.

ALEXANDRA STODDARD

A Record Mile Run

I can do all things through Him
who strengthens me.

PHILIPPIANS 4:13

One evening my grandson Chad, who was in the sixth grade at the time, called and wanted to know which verse of Scripture said that a person could do all things. After I thought for a few moments, this passage came to mind. I asked Chad why he needed to know. He replied that tomorrow he was running the mile for the Presidential Physical Fitness Certificate, and he was really nervous about this event. He said his stomach was churning and he wasn't going to be able to sleep, which would cause him to be tired tomorrow. He was worried he wouldn't do well.

He wanted to read this verse so he could be at ease and do a good job in the race. We talked for a while. I had a word of prayer with him and hung up the phone. The next morning I called to see how he had slept, and he assured me he was good and rested. He also said his mom had prepared him a high-energy breakfast. He was off to school with confidence that he would do his very best.

That afternoon the phone rang, and Chad was on the other end telling me with a cheerful voice, "Grammy, I won the race in record time. I know that the verse and your prayers really helped me. I will always remember that verse when I need reassurance. Thanks, Grammy."

What a thrill for me to realize that a 12-year-old boy went to Scripture to help him in life. And what a reminder that I need to do the same in every situation. Where do you run when you are worried and need help? Trust more and more of your life and your responsibilities to God's strength. You will discover the amazing things He has planned for you.

❈ Prayer ❈

Father God, I do know that I can do all things through Christ. He is my strength and my assurance. He helps me when things are tough. I'm so thankful that I can run to You with my every need and concern. You don't turn me away. You embrace me and show me the way. Thank You. Amen.

❈ Heart Action ❈

Share your concerns with God today. And when

you are done, share your joys and praises with Him too.

The grandfather plants and raises the tea bushes,
the father harvests the tea,
and the son drinks it.

CHINESE SAYING

Finding Complete Happiness

Enter His gates with thanksgiving
And His courts with praise.
Give thanks to Him, bless His name.

—Psalm 100:4

"If only I could take a shopping cart to my favorite store and shop until I had all the stuff I wanted—then I would be happy!" Have you echoed that thought before?

I had a very close friend who often said aloud, "If only I could have a bigger house, a bigger car, a bigger ring, live in a certain city—then I would be happy." After 25 years she is still looking for happiness in possessions. How sad to watch her spiral downward into depression because she's always looking for happiness in the wrong places.

The Scriptures are quite clear that a thankful heart is a happy heart. To have complete happiness we must enter into the Lord's presence with thanksgiving. I have found in my own life that when I am appreciative for all I have, my mental, physical, and spiritual dimensions are at balance with each other. The family chores run more smoothly, and the mood of my home is more relaxed. I'm excited to bounce out of bed each day challenged by what may come my way. During this time of peace and tranquility, my friends seem to bond closer to me. I'm fun to be around. There is an air of positiveness that is transmitted from my presence. People like to be around people who are positive and edifying.

When we start our day with a heart of gratitude and look for reasons to be joyful rather than reasons to complain, our days will unfold in a positive direction. When we build up instead of tear down, we will see the people around us blossom and shine. When we take our eyes off of stuff and become women of thanksgiving, we will be more focused on people, love, health, blessings, and God. When we are thankful, possessions will be in proper perspective and happiness will not elude us.

❋ PRAYER ❋

Father God, take away my focus on acquiring things. Let me be a person with a thankful heart. I know my happiness does not depend upon me acquiring possessions.

Help me break away from this materialism.
I do thank You for all I have. Amen.

❧ HEART ACTION ❧

Take time tonight around the dinner table to express thanks for all that God has given you and your family. And remember the little things too.

Thank God for tea!
What would the world do without tea?
How did it exist?
I am glad I was not born before tea.

REVEREND SYDNEY SMITH

Be Willing to
Say "Thank You!"

Love is patient, love is kind and is not jealous;
love does not brag and is not arrogant.

—1 Corinthians 13:4

As fellow believers, we must be sensitive to the fact that we don't want to take our spouses for granted. After many years of marriage, my Bob and I continue to work on this area of our life. We continue to do little courtesies for each other. He is such a gracious gentleman wherever we go. Women often comment to me what a warm, soft, and tender man he is. He still opens my car door and lets me enter buildings first. He brings me flowers and takes me to special shows. He asks me rather than tells me, considers me equal to him, and is willing to seek and hear my opinion. He is always ready to say thank you.

Likewise, I'm continually extending my appreciation to my Bob. I never want to be void of my thankfulness for him as my husband. Taking a mate for granted is one of the main reasons our country experiences a 50-percent divorce rate, with a higher percentage for second and third marriages. Don't get caught in the trap of expecting your mate to do so-and-so just because he is your spouse.

As the years fly by, Bob and I continually discuss our feelings toward each other. Are we still filling each other's "emotional tanks," or are we drifting into complacency? Have you stopped to ask your spouse what you can do for him? Have you shared your needs with him through gentle conversation rather than through complaining? Open up the communication lines so you can be a support and helpmate to your husband and so you can accept and lean on the help he gives you.

Appreciation is your choosing; choose today to stop taking your spouse for granted. Get excited about life and its many challenges. Choose to be grateful and to express your appreciation. The more you do, the easier it becomes.

You will have a fuller and richer life when you focus on thankfulness.

❀ PRAYER ❀

Lord, don't let me become complacent about my mate. I want to always be an encourager. Thank You for the love of my

husband and for the role this relationship
plays in helping me develop into the
woman You want me to become. Amen.

❧ HEART ACTION ❧

Take time to tell your spouse what you love most about him. Express your thankfulness for the big and small things.

Cook, cook, drink your tea
But save some in the pot for me...

UNKNOWN

Tea for Plenty

When you are preparing tea for a large group, you can brew this concentrate up to two hours ahead and still serve hot, perfect tea. This recipe makes about 50 cups of tea, but you can make more or less concentrate according to your needs. Remember: To make tea in quantity, don't brew longer—use more tea.

- 1½ cups loose tea or 16 family-size tea bags
- 2½ quarts boiling water

Pour boiling water over tea in large non-metallic container. Let steep for 5 minutes, then strain the tea leaves or remove tea bags. Store concentrate at room temperature until needed. To serve, use 2 tablespoons of concentrate per 5-ounce cup—or about 3 parts of water to every part concentrate. Place the desired amount of the concentrate in a cup or pot and then add the hot water. Note: This concentrate also makes delicious iced tea. Put 4 tablespoons in an 8-ounce glass of water, then add water and ice.

FILLED STRAWBERRIES

These fresh-fruit treats are like strawberry cheesecakes in miniature—perfect for a tea. Whip 6 ounces of room-temperature cream cheese on medium speed until slightly puffy, 2 to 3 minutes. Add ½ teaspoon pure vanilla extract and 1½ tablespoons confectioner's sugar. Trim tops and bottoms of 12 strawberries to level. Use a small melon baller to scoop out strawberries. Fill a pastry bag fitted with ½-inch star tip with cream cheese mixture; pipe into berries until it brims over tops. Toast ¼ cup sliced almonds in a 350° F oven until golden brown, 3 to 6 minutes; arrange almonds on top of the filling.

❋ ❋ ❋

I always fear that creation will
expire before teatime.

REVEREND SYDNEY SMITH

What You Can't Do Can Be Fun

A faithful [woman] will abound with blessings.

—PROVERBS 28:20

Have you ever met people with limited income who are rich, or rich people who are poor? I certainly have, and I love to see how different people stretch their money to become wealthy. I have a very good friend who can make a silk purse out of a sow's ear. She just knows how to shop. She lives in a very affluent area of Southern California, so she takes great delight in going into second-time-around stores to purchase very nice clothing at greatly reduced prices. Another friend has made her rental condo into a dollhouse. She takes old furniture and gives it the latest artistic touch, and she adds a few touches with fabric accents she makes on her sewing machine. My Bob used to have a barber whose wife loved to drive a Lincoln Town Car, but they couldn't afford one on his income. They would watch the ads and rent one for the weekend. That was just enough to satisfy her desire to drive a large car.

Another couple I know loves to camp along the California coastline. For very little cost they will visit a different state park each year and have a wonderful time with their family. They—and you—can find happiness within a budget.

Don't spend time thinking about what you don't have, but count your blessings for the things you do have. Don't wait until the next big raise to do something more than you are used to. Instead, find happiness where you are. Make the best and most of what you have. One way to minimize the stress over a tight budget is to make the decision to stop using a lack of funds to justify your unhappiness. This isn't an "if only I had" world. Enjoy what you have as much as possible.

❖ PRAYER ❖

Father God, You have given me more than
I could ever thank You for. As a young girl I
never thought I would be so blessed. Let me
continue to enjoy what I can't do, and let me
shout "thank You" for what I have. Amen.

❖ HEART ACTION ❖

Do something fun this weekend that costs little

or no money. Think about the ways that you are rich in spirit and love.

> *The Baroness found it amusing to go to tea;*
> *she dressed as if for dinner. The tea-table offered*
> *an anomalous and picturesque repast; and on*
> *leaving it they all sat and*
> *talked in the large piazza, or wandered*
> *about the garden in the starlight.*

HENRY JAMES

Home Robbers

*The worries of the world, and the deceitfulness
of riches, and the desires for other things enter in
and choke the word, and it becomes unfruitful.*

—MARK 4:19

If we're not on guard, the things of the world
will enter into our homes and rob us of contentment. We get trapped in "we need this"; "we don't
have enough of that"; "if only my kitchen was bigger";
"my dishes are so old"; "I don't have the right wall
paper"; "the cupboards need a fresh coat of paint"; "I
can't entertain until I have new carpet"; and so on.
Do these joy-robbing phrases sound familiar? Have
you uttered a few of them?

I encourage you to take a moment to be refreshed.
Instead of focusing on a home beautiful, contemplate
a home filled with the spirit of loveliness—the spirit
of warmth and caring. I talk with hundreds of women
like you who truly have a heart for home. Your situation
may be unusual, but like most women you probably
want to be a home builder, not a home robber.

Do you long for a home that is warm and welcoming, comfortable and freeing? A place where you can express the uniqueness of your God-given talents and nurture your relationships with people you love? Do you desire a home that reflects your personality and renews your soul—a place that glows with a spirit of loveliness? I believe this spirit is already in your heart. You *can* stop the home robbers at the curb and not allow them to enter.

No matter how little or how much you have, you can experience the results of having a godly home. Take steps toward making your home a sanctuary— a place of security, trust, and comfort. A place to be reenergized, pray, and dream. You can begin with a friendly welcome at the front door for your family and friends.

❀ PRAYER ❀

Father God, there are so many people who want to steal the joy of my home. May I cast away those acquaintances who are negative in thought. I want to cherish my family and friends who build up my desire to reflect Your spirit of loveliness in my home. Amen.

❋ Heart Action ❋

Spend time being refreshed. Read God's Word. Sip a cup of tea. Relax in a comfy chair that gets a bit of afternoon sun. Reflect on the goodness of life.

Real joy comes not from ease or riches
or from the praise of men, but from
doing something worthwhile.

Wilfred T. Grenfell

Praise Is Good and Pleasant

God is spirit, and those who worship Him must worship in spirit and truth.

—JOHN 4:24

The date September 11, 2001, was a historic day in America's spiritual awakening. This was the day when, at 8:45 on a Tuesday morning, carefully planned acts of terrorism demolished the World Trade Center in New York, damaged the Pentagon in Washington, D.C., and ended in destruction in rural Pennsylvania. Thousands of lives were lost.

In the days following, our country experienced a great spiritual outpouring. Churches and synagogues overflowed with people who wanted to praise God publicly. They cried, prayed, sang songs, read Scripture, and heard pastors and teachers give messages on why evil exists in our world. Television and radio programs were eager to cover these gatherings throughout the world. United praise is good.

Psalm 150 reads:

Praise the LORD! Praise God in His sanctuary; praise Him in His mighty expanse. Praise Him for His mighty deeds; praise Him according to His excellent greatness.

Praise Him with trumpet sound; praise Him with harp and lyre. Praise Him with timbrel and dancing; praise Him with stringed instruments and pipe. Praise Him with loud cymbals; praise Him with resounding cymbals. Let everything that has breath praise the LORD. Praise the LORD!

While single praise is good, united praise is like music in concert. There is nothing so pleasant to our ears, heart, and soul as to be a part of the body of Christ coming together in congregational praise. When I hear these joined voices it makes me wonder what heaven will be like when all the angelic voices join together in great praise and worship.

There is something delightful in the union of true hearts in worship of God, especially when these hearts of praise are being expressed in song.

❧ PRAYER ❧

Father God, just to think about the united singing of praises to You gives me goose

*bumps. There is nothing so wonderful as to
be a part of a chorus praising You in song.
I look forward to every worship service
at church when we as a body of believers
lift our voices to praise You. Amen.*

❋ HEART ACTION ❋

Join with another person today in prayer. Lift up
the nation. Lift up the world.

> *To beat fatigue
> you'll all agree,
> There's nothing like
> a cup of tea.*

UNKNOWN

The Humble Shall Hear

David was dancing before the
LORD with all his might.

—2 SAMUEL 6:14

When we have prayer that is answered, we should always follow it with praise. When the Lord has been gracious to our prayers, we should praise Him! Don't be silent; those around you need to hear of God's grace to you. As I have had so many of my prayers answered, I want to be the first to thank God in public for all He's done. My favorite Scripture during the dark period of illness in my life was John 11:4, which reads, "This sickness is not to end in death, but for the glory of God, that the Son of God may be glorified by it."

Praise is a healthy exercise; it is the most heavenly of our Christian duties. When we praise God for answered prayers, we benefit our fellow believers: "The humble shall hear thereof, and be glad" (Psalm 34:2 KJV).

Don't be a silent Christian—be willing to sing and give praises to God.

The great doxology of the church written by Thomas Ken took these words—

> Praise God, from whom all blessings flow,
> Praise Him all creatures here below,
>
> Praise Him above ye heavenly host,
> Praise Father, Son, and Holy Ghost. Amen.

—and made them ring out each Sunday in many of our churches. These words recognize that as the creatures of God's creation we are to praise our magnificent God. In Psalm 109:30 we read, "With my mouth I will give thanks abundantly to the LORD; and in the midst of many I will praise Him."

We are to be in a state of continuous praise to God for what He has done in our lives. He is everything to us: our healer, our provider, our comforter, our Savior, our redeemer, our security.

❉ PRAYER ❉

Father God, I am encouraged when I hear from others how gracious You have been in their lives. May all of us stand and be noted as ones who are thankful. Help us to not let bashfulness stop us from sharing. Amen.

❃ HEART ACTION ❃

Think about when you are silent about God's activity in your life. Look for a chance this week to speak out about God's goodness.

Giving and gratitude go together like humor and laughter, like having one's back rubbed and the sigh that follows, like a blowing wind and the murmur of wind chimes. Gratitude keeps alive the rhythm of grace given and grace grateful, a lively lilt that lightens a heavy world.

LEWIS B. SMEDES

Give Us This Day

*Our Father who is in heaven, hallowed be
Your name. Your kingdom come. Your will
be done, on earth as it is in heaven. Give us
this day our daily bread. And forgive us our
debts, as we also have forgiven our debtors.
And do not lead us into temptation, but
deliver us from evil. For Yours is the kingdom
and the power and the glory forever. Amen.*

—Matthew 6:9-13

The "Lord's Prayer" is a model for our prayers. It begins with adoration of God (verse 9), acknowledges subjection to His will (verse 10), asks of Him (verses 11-13), and ends with an offering of praise (verse 13).

The fatherhood of God toward His children is the basis for Jesus' frequent teaching about prayer. "Your Father knows what you need," Jesus told His disciples, "before you ask Him" (Matthew 6:8). Jesus presents a pattern that the church has followed throughout the centuries.

Prayer begins by honoring the name of God. He

is worthy of honor because He is the heavenly King, yet His rule is being extended over the earth as well. Because He is King, we can entrust all our physical needs to His provision, asking Him to "give us our food for today," instead of worrying about the future.

Since God is our merciful Father, we also seek forgiveness from Him while we forgive those who have sinned against us. Finally, we ask our Father to keep us from yielding to temptation and to deliver us from the evil one, for our God is able to defeat any evil that comes against us.

This model of prayer is one that should be engraved upon our hearts—and the hearts of the children God has given us. Information stored in our memory bank can't be taken from us.

❊ Prayer ❊

Lord, Your model prayer has come to me in the night on several occasions and has given me great comfort. Your prayer has become my prayer, and I enjoy reciting it often when I think of You. Amen.

❊ Heart Action ❊

Trust the Lord each day for your provision.

Let me live according to those holy rules which thou hast this day prescribed in thy holy word; make me to know what is acceptable in thy holy word; make me to know what is acceptable in thy sight, and therein to delight, open the eyes of my understanding, and help me thoroughly to examine myself concerning my knowledge, faith and repentance, increase my faith, and direct me to the true object, Jesus Christ, the way, the truth and the life.

GEORGE WASHINGTON

EMILIE'S INSPIRED POT OF TEA

Preparing a perfect cup of tea takes time, but the flavor and excellence is worth it!

1. Fill a teakettle with freshly drawn cold water. Put the kettle on to boil.

2. While the kettle is heating, pour hot water into the teapot to warm it. Ceramic (china, porcelain, stoneware) or glass teapots work best; tea brewed in metal may have a metallic taste.

3. Pour the hot water out of the teapot and add the tea. Measure a spoonful of loose tea for each cup desired into the warmed (empty) teapot, plus 1 extra spoonful for the pot. (Most teapots hold 5 to 6 cups.) If you are using tea bags, use one bag less than the desired number of cups. Put the lid back on.

4. As soon as the kettle comes to a rolling boil, remove from heat. Overboiling causes the water to lose oxygen, and the resulting brew will taste flat.

5. Pour boiling water into the teapot, cover, and let the tea brew from 3 to 6 minutes. Small tea leaves will take less time to brew than large ones.

6. Gently stir the tea before pouring it through a tea strainer into the teacups. If you used tea bags, remove them.

THE CARE OF A TEAPOT

In previous centuries, protecting precious tea ware was the responsibility of the house-keeper, who stored it in her sitting room "below stairs." She oversaw the tea supply, brewed tea for "above stairs," and washed the fragile tea china. The best method was, and is, to rinse the teapot with warm water (no soap) and let it air dry. Tannin buildup vanishes when the pot is gently scrubbed with a wet cloth dipped in baking soda or by filling the pot with soda and warm water, and soaking. A lump of sugar in the teapot absorbs moisture and keeps it smelling fresh.

You Don't Always Have to Win

*The anger of man does not achieve
the righteousness of God.*

—James 1:20

I don't know about you, but I have never won an argument. Even though my Bob might say, "I give, you win!" my heart feels heavy and certainly not victorious. It certainly doesn't feel like we've been drawn together. In fact, disagreements drive us farther apart. When disagreements arise, the interaction between the parties can be far from ideal.

An argument is when two or more parties are trying to prove their positions. Very seldom does anyone listen to learn anything; each party is trying to overpower his or her opponent with oratory or volume. Rarely do people feel good in this situation. There are usually feelings of resentment, anger, frustration, and stress.

However, if you allow someone else to win a disagreement, it's often the case that both of you are winners. It's often a very rewarding experience that allows your relationship to grow. When you let someone else win, you are showing that it's no big deal to always be right. I know this can be a difficult assignment because in our competitive society we are taught that winning is everything.

When you are willing to let someone else win, you will find yourself better able to listen because you aren't trying to overpower the other person with your opinion.

Yes, there are some critical positions that must be defended, but those are usually few in life. These points must be defended because of your moral and biblical position.

Here are several key verses dealing with anger that help us understand the process outlined in Scripture:

- "A quick-tempered man acts foolishly" (Proverbs 14:17).

- "A gentle answer turns away wrath, but a harsh word stirs up anger" (Proverbs 15:1).

- "Everyone must be quick to hear, slow to speak and slow to anger" (James 1:19).

- "Do not let the sun go down on your anger" (Ephesians 4:26).

❊ Prayer ❊

*Father God, I appreciate that You have given
me the ability to let someone else win an
argument. It's okay not to always be right, and I
don't feel any less a person because I also benefit.
I don't have to "win" to be content. Amen.*

❊ Heart Action ❊

Give in during an argument in order to experience that peace and victory. And the next time you want to start an argument, talk yourself out of it. Give the issue to God and allow your anger or your need to be right to subside.

Listen

*Everyone must be quick to hear, slow
to speak and slow to anger.*

—James 1:19

God in His great wisdom created mankind with two ears and only one mouth. I'm sure that was because He wanted us to listen twice as much as we speak. Most of us are very poor listeners. Bob and I rate this skill as one of the top priorities in having a good relationship. I guarantee that if couples would take the time to become better listeners, their relationships would be improved through better understanding and increased patience. (It's important to remember, though, that women tend to be better listeners than men, probably because most men immediately want to fix what is broken and consider listening a waste of time. To them, the solution is what's important; they want to go directly to the bottom line.)

So be brave and ask several of your trusted friends how they would rate you on your listening skills. Be prepared to take their honest answers and act upon the information constructively. Don't get into the trap of thinking you are much better at listening than so-and-so. Almost everyone is below par in this skill.

We will become better listeners when we realize how people value being heard. It gives people an awareness that we care for what they have to say and that we truly love them. Our own spirits are lifted up when those around us know we care for them.

Listening is truly an art form that can be mastered if we practice. Observe yourself in a crowd, or even one-on-one, to see how you do. Change comes when you know the truth.

❋ Prayer ❋

Father God, how precious it is to listen to another one of Your children. Give me an ear to hear the needs that are spoken and unspoken by the people around me. Help me to not be in such a hurry that I miss the chance to engage in conversation or to pray for another. Amen.

❋ Heart Action ❋

Listen to your husband, your child, your friends, and to strangers with an attentive, caring mind and a compassionate, open heart. You'll discover how much more you truly hear!

Stands the church clock at ten to three?
And is there honey for the tea?

RUPERT BROOKE

An Invitation to Tea

*My dear, if you could give me a cup
of tea to clear my muddle of a head I
should better understand your affairs.*

CHARLES DICKENS

If teacups could talk, my house would be full of conversation…because my house is full of teacups. My collection of china cups—begun many years ago, when I set up housekeeping as a child bride—has long since outgrown its home in the glass-front armoire and spread out to occupy side tables and shelves and hooks in the kitchen or find safe harbor in the dining-room hutch.

Some of these cups I inherited from women I love—my mother and my aunties. Some are gifts from my husband, Bob, or from my children or from special friends. A few are delightful finds from elegant boutiques or dusty antique shops.

One cup bears telltale cracks and scars; it was the only one I could salvage when a shelf slipped and 14 cups fell and shattered.

Three other cups stand out for their intense color—my aunt was always attracted to that kind of dramatic decoration.

Yet another cup, a gift, is of a style I've never much cared for, but now it makes me smile as I remember the houseguest who "rescued" it from a dark corner of the armoire because it looked "lonely."

Each one of my teacups has a history, and each one is precious to me. I have gladly shared them with guests and told their stories to many people.

Recently, however, I have been more inclined to listen.

I've been wondering what all those cups, with their history and long experience, are trying to say to *me*.

What I hear from them, over and over, is an invitation—one I want to extend to you: When did you last have a tea party? When was the last time you enjoyed a cup of tea with someone you care about? Isn't it time you did it again?

❈ PRAYER ❈

Lord, You invite me to Your presence.
Here I discover such peace and comfort and
hospitality. May I discover how to share these
same gifts with others—neighbors, friends,

family, and strangers. Lord, help me to see
those You bring into my life. Give me a heart
for all people and a willingness to serve and
love them. I will embrace each day as an
opportunity to embrace the heart of tea and
to listen carefully to Your leading. Amen.

❀ Heart Action ❀

Plan a tea party to gather together some old or new friends. Even having just one person over for a cup of tea and good conversation will create a time of hospitality and connection. Make it simple so that you enjoy it and can focus on sharing your heart with your guests.

A Tea Party Has Its Own Manners

Serving tea is a wonderful excuse for sharpening etiquette around the table. Mothers can use this time to teach their young daughters about the importance of learning and practicing good manners.

- The server of teas and all liquids will serve from the right. The person being served will hold their cups in the left hand. You may adjust this if the person receiving is left-handed.

- To prevent from getting lipstick on your teacup, blot your lipstick before you sit down at the serving table.

- Scones and crumpets should be eaten in small bite-sized pieces. If butter, jam, or cream is used, add them to each piece as it is eaten.

- Good manners will dictate proper conversation. The goodies are theatre, museums, fine arts, music, movies, literature, and travel. The baddies are politics, religion, aches and pains, deaths, and negative discussion. Keep the conversation upbeat.

- A knife and fork are usually used with open-faced sandwiches and cakes with icing.

- Milk or cream is always added after the tea is poured.
- The placing of the napkin tells the waiter or host the progress of your enjoyment. When you are leaving the table for a brief period, the napkin is placed on the seat of the chair. At the end of your tea, the napkin is folded and placed on the table.
- After being hosted for a lovely tea, always write a pleasant thank-you note. E-mails are not acceptable.
- Cell-phone ringers are always placed in the off position while enjoying a delightful tea.

A Loving Recipe for a Perfect Cup of Tea

- 1 willing friend who loves to sit and share
- 1 grateful heart to have a friend that cares
- 1 beautiful garden to show us God is near

The Secret of the Wise Man

You desire truth in the innermost being, and in the hidden part You will make me know wisdom.

—Psalm 51:6

Recently I was driving down one of our busy freeways in Southern California, when a sign suddenly appeared before me that read, "What the fool does at the end, wise men do at the beginning." I don't know how I was able to glimpse this since I was driving by, but my mind affirmed that this slogan has so much meaning.

We live in a day when humanity has sold out to secular materialism, a day when many people have put God on hold. The attitude of "I can do it myself; I don't need help from anyone—especially from a God I can't see or touch" rules. But as time goes on, many older people seem to get more wisdom after they have found that their paths have given them little meaning in life. As they ponder mortality, they often realize that the simplicity of their youth offered a peace and meaning they rejected all through life. Wise people, on the other hand, have adopted the fear of God at a young age. They have studied the wisdom of Scripture and applied it to their value structure.

Wisdom comes from knowing God and understanding His will for our lives. The Holy Spirit assists us in our quest for wisdom by enabling us to view the world as God perceives it. From an early age we can seek God's wisdom. We don't have to wait until we are old to figure out this puzzle of life. In Psalm 111:10 we read, "The fear of the LORD is the beginning of wisdom; a good understanding have all those who do His commandments; His praise endures forever."

Don't put off until tomorrow what you can do today. A wasted lifetime is a shame. Go to the cross of Jesus and trust Him with the simplicity of childlike faith.

❋ PRAYER ❋

Father God, I don't want to wait until I'm very old to exhibit Your traits of wisdom. I want a whole life of trusting You and Your Word. May I also be able to transmit this desire to my family. Bless me as I put my faith into Your hands. Amen.

❉ HEART ACTION ❉

Decide what you need help with today. Give that specifically to God. And allow yourself to ask for help from others. It's a big step but an important one. Your chance to help someone else will be just around the corner. Learn to receive and give with great faith.

Kindness is more important than
wisdom, and the recognition of this
is the beginning of wisdom.

THEODORE RUBIN

Make a Date
with Yourself

There is an appointed time for everything. And there is a time for every event under heaven.

—ECCLESIASTES 3:1

What would we do without our day planners? I have a large one for my desk and a carry-all that goes with me. I don't know how a person functions without some type of organizer. I just love it; it truly has become my daily-calendar bible. I take it with me everywhere. My whole life is in that book. Each evening I peek in to see what tomorrow has to bring. I just love to see a busy calendar; it makes me feel so alive. I've got this to do and that to do.

Then I come upon a day that has all white space. Not one thing to do. *What, oh what, will I do to fill the space and time?* That's the way I used to think and plan. All my spaces had appointments written down, and many times they even overlapped.

I now plan for white spaces. I even plan ahead weeks or months and black out "saved for me or my family" days. I have begun to realize that there are precious times for myself and my loved ones. Bob and I really try to protect these saved spaces just for us. We may not go anywhere or do anything out of the ordinary, but it's our special time. We can do anything we want: sleep in, stay out late, go to lunch, read a book, go to a movie, or take a nap. I really look forward with great anticipation to when these white spaces appear on my calendar.

I've been so impressed when I've read biographies of famous people. Many of them are controllers of their own time. They don't let outsiders dictate their schedules. Sure, there are times when things have to be done on special days, but generally that isn't the case. When we begin to control our calendars, we will find that our lives are more enjoyable and that the tensions of life are more manageable. Make those white spaces your friend, not your enemy.

❋ Prayer ❋

Father God, I am working to make room in my life for more of the things that please You. I want my daily activities, priorities, and choices to reflect my love for You and my commitment to You. Give me a discerning mind so that I make space for

*family, prayer, devotion, worship, and
caring for others and myself. Amen.*

❋ HEART ACTION ❋

Take back control of your time and your days.
Flip to your calendar and make three white spaces
just for you. You'll be on your way to a new sense of
freedom and peace.

*The effect of tea is cooling and as a beverage
it is most suitable. It is especially fitting for
persons of self-restraint and inner worth.*

LU YU

Life Is More Than Abundance

Beware, and be on your guard against every form of greed; for not even when one has an abundance does his life consist of his possessions.

—LUKE 12:15

One of our universal problems is the overcrowding of our homes. Whether we have an apartment or a six-bedroom home, every closet, cupboard, refrigerator, and garage are all crammed with abundance. Some of us have so much that we go out and rent additional storage spaces for our possessions.

Bob and I are no different than you. We buy new clothes and cram them into our wardrobes. A new antique goes in the corner, a new quilt hangs over the bed, a new potted plant gathers sunlight by the window. On and on it goes. Pretty soon we feel as though we are closed in with no room to breathe. We continually struggle to keep a balance in our attitudes regarding possessions.

It is simpler to manage if you are single and

live alone—it's just you. Life becomes more complicated with a spouse and children. You soon get that "bunched in" feeling. This creates more stress, and you can lose your cool and blow relationships when your calm is broken.

We have made a rule in our home about abundance. Simply stated, it says, "One comes in and one goes out." After every purchase we give away or sell a like item. (We have an annual garage sale.) With a new blouse, out goes an older blouse; with a new table, out goes a table; and so on. Naturally if you're a newlywed this rule is not for you because you probably don't have an abundance of possessions.

There's another strategy that's very effective. We have informed our loved ones that we don't want any more gifts that take up space or that have to be dusted; we prefer receiving consumable items Remember—your life is not based on your possessions. Share with others what you aren't using.

❊ PRAYER ❊

Father God, help me incorporate this new principle in my life. I don't want to be stressed out in this life because I own too much. Let me learn to be a giver and not a taker of possessions. I need help in this area of my life. Amen.

❊ Heart Action ❊

What can you get rid of today or this week? Get rid of it and don't replace it!

All you're supposed to do is every once in a while give the boys a little tea and sympathy.

Robert Anderson

Vanilla Milk Tea

This blend is a perfect introduction for children or for people who aren't accustomed to drinking tea. Use less milk if the drinker would like a stronger blend of tea. Use a vanilla bean, or stir in 2 teaspoons of pure vanilla extract into each cup of milk. Makes 4-5 cups.

- 1 cup milk
- 2-inch piece of vanilla bean, split
- 4 teaspoons English Breakfast tea
- 1 quart boiling water

Pour the milk in a small saucepan, add the vanilla bean, and bring to a simmer, stirring often. Remove the pan from the heat and let it stand until the milk is cool. Remove the bean from the pan. Warm a teapot and cups with hot water. Drain and dry them. Put tea leaves in the teapot, add boiling water, cover with a cozy or towel, and let steep for 5 minutes. Pour about ¼ cup of cooled milk into teacups. Stir and strain the tea into the hot cups. Serve right away.

DELICIOUS BUTTER COOKIES

- 1 pound butter
- 1 cup granulated sugar
- 1 beaten egg
- 1 pound flour (4 cups)
- ¼ teaspoon salt
- 1 tablespoon vanilla

Cream butter and sugar gradually. Add beaten egg to this mixture. Sift flour and salt together and add to mixture. Stir thoroughly. Then add vanilla and mix. Drop dough from teaspoon onto greased cookie sheet. Bake at 350° F for 20 to 25 minutes. May be decorated as desired before baking. May also be put through a cookie press. Makes 36.

One Who Walks in Integrity

A righteous [woman] who walks in [her] integrity—how blessed are [her] sons after [her].

—PROVERBS 20:7

My Bob often says, "Just do what you say you are going to do!" This has been our battle cry for more than 25 years. People get into relational problems because they forget to keep their promises. It's so easy to make a verbal promise for the moment and then grapple with the execution of that promise later.

Sometimes we underestimate the consequences of not keeping the promise flippantly made in a moment of haste. Many times we aren't even aware we have made a promise. Someone says, "I'll call you at 7:00 tonight"; "I'll drop by before noon"; or "I'll call you to set up a breakfast meeting on Wednesday." Then the weak excuses begin to follow. "I called but no one answered" (even though you have voice mail and no message was left). "I got tied up and forgot." "I was too tired."

I suggest that we don't make promises if we aren't going to keep them. The person on the other end would prefer not hearing a promise that isn't going to be kept.

Yes, there will be times when the execution of a promise will have to be rescheduled, but be up front with the person when you call to change the time. We aren't perfect, but we can mentor proper relationship skills to our friends and family by exhibiting accountability in our words of promise. We teach people that we are trustworthy—and how they can be trusted too.

You'll be pleased at how people will pleasantly be surprised when you keep your promises. As my friend Florence Littauer says, "It takes so little to be above average." When you develop a reputation for being a woman who does what she says, your life will have more meaning and people will enjoy being around you.

❧ PRAYER ❧

Father God, I want to be a person that others can trust when I make a promise. Let me examine my words to make sure I only give promises to others when I'm committed to fulfill what I've uttered. Truly, keeping

promises reflects on my Christian witness.
Convict me to be true to my words. Amen.

❄ HEART ACTION ❄

Practice integrity in all that you say and do. Work on making promises only when you are certain you will keep them. Become a woman that others can trust.

Drinking a daily cup of tea will
surely starve the apothecary.

CHINESE PROVERB

That Inner Feeling

The LORD has done what He purposed;
He has accomplished His word.

—LAMENTATIONS 2:17

I often have an instinctive feeling that something isn't right, that I should do this or that, but I usually pass over this because peer pressure tells me my inner feelings should be ignored. The older I become, however, the more I realize that living from my heart has value.

I don't want to get into the trap of following everyone else because it's the group thing to do. I want to live a life that is meaningful to me and my family. I want my decisions to be based on my Christian values. To help me make major decisions, I want to use these values, not what TV, Madison Avenue, or popular newsstand magazines tell me to do or think.

In order to live intuitively one must have some quiet times to read and think. Hectic lives don't permit one to hear the heartbeat of the soul. When we are too busy we don't have time to dwell on the important issues in life.

I find that when I'm rushed I have an inner disturbance that prevents me from making well-thought-out decisions. When you and I are hurried, we have a tendency to have a deep anger inside because we forget to have time for ourselves. Our personal growth comes to a standstill.

When I faced downtime during my battle with cancer, I was able to reflect upon the important issues of life. God has taught me to read, think, and dwell upon what my heart knows to be true. I'm more in tune now with the beat of my heart.

❖ Prayer ❖

Father God, let me be more aware of the feelings of my heart. You have given me so many of the desires of my heart, and I want to be more sensitive to what You are teaching me about life. I search for a solitude of peace and tranquility so I can hear Your thoughts in my heart. Amen.

❖ Heart Action ❖

Find the calmer pace of your heart and soul. Take time to listen to your heart so you can discover the truths it holds about yourself, your faith, and your Creator.

*Each cup of tea
represents an imaginary voyage.*

CATHERINE DOUZEL

Castles in the Sand

No man can lay a foundation other than the
one which is laid, which is Jesus Christ.

—1 CORINTHIANS 3:11

Each Independence Day the city of Newport Beach, California, sponsors a huge sand-castle-building contest. Our family has had the opportunity to observe this spectacle for several years. Men, women, and children arrive early with shovels, buckets, and trowels in hand to spend the whole day sculpting magnificent structures out of sand. It's absolutely amazing to watch the teamwork that goes on. Each person seems to know what to do next. One of the hardest jobs is to go to the water's edge and bring back buckets of water to put on the sand structure. (Wet sand is a must.) The creative team members are the sculptors who take a pile of sand and begin to form their sand-castle vision. Medieval castles with turrets, drawbridges, and protective moats are very popular. As the judges take their positions, the crowd waits with anticipation. Who will be the winners?

The last few hours of the day are spent watching

the beautiful creations. That is, until the tide begins to advance and the waves nibble at these gorgeous structures until they are all flattened and washed back into the ocean.

This is a great reminder for us to make sure that our efforts here on earth are everlasting—made with the gold, silver, and precious stones of our hearts and not with the perishable materials of wood, hay, and straw.

❋ PRAYER ❋

Father God, I want my life to mean more than building castles in the sand. I know they look beautiful, but I also realize they aren't eternal in nature. Help me to discern what is everlasting so I will live on in the eyes of my children and grandchildren because of what was of value to me. Amen.

❋ HEART ACTION ❋

Build with lasting materials. Keep your perspective on the eternal as you nurture relationships and make decisions for your life.

❋ COME ONE, COME ALL ❋

A good friend of mine has a freshly painted sign

that reads, "Join me for tea at THREE." That sign posted in her yard lets all of her neighbors know that they are invited to come and enjoy tea with her at three. Of course, this isn't a full-blown tea, but Sheri does have a few sweets and a variety of teas to choose from. This has been a great way for the neighbor ladies to get to know each other.

Three Sweet Words

*Beloved, let us love one another, for love
is from God; and everyone who loves
is born of God and knows God.*

—1 John 4:7

Have you ever hungered after love?

When my father, who was an alcoholic, was alive, I would hope that he would come home with love in his heart rather than the anger he often exhibited. As a young girl I would have so cherished those three big words, "I love you." I guess that's one of the first reasons I was so attracted to my Bob. He came from a warm family that was very free in their expressions of endearment.

Over the years I, too, have made it a habit to say, "I love you." Saying these difficult words (I say difficult because the world finds them so hard to utter) has been very beneficial to me: It helps me feel good inside; it makes me realize that I'm a giver and not just a taker.

When our loved ones hear these words they certainly erase all the mistakes we've made recently. I often catch myself saying, "I love you," as I hang up from talking to a friend or family member. You know what? After a while they return the forgotten words "I love you." There are many opportunities during the day to express that precious sentence.

Individuals who know they are loved have a cheerier outlook on life. There is a sparkle in their eyes, and they can look you in the eye with a face that reflects confidence. This inner peace will radiate in all of their relationships. It is most difficult to not like someone who says that they love you. In fact it is almost impossible to do so.

The Scriptures are quite clear that God is love, and when we don't love we can't know God intimately. How often have we known a person for just a short time and realized that we are kindred spirits? Why? Because he or she radiates the love of God. God's light truly shines.

❧ PRAYER ❧

Father God, may I be known by those around me as being a person who knows how to say, "I love you." May my family never be able to accuse me of not telling them I love them. I want to freely give these words to those I know. Amen.

Write down the ways that God shows His love to you. It will be a reminder of how you are loved and also a good list of ways that you can show love to others.

The path to heaven passes through a teapot.

ANCIENT PROVERB

Examine Your Heart

And I will give them one heart, and
put a new spirit within them.
And I will take the heart of stone out of
their flesh and give them a heart of flesh.

—Ezekiel 11:19

An engine with all its cylinders working properly can propel a large truck to its destination; a neglected engine may not be able to move a vehicle out of the parking lot. So it is with the people of God. Worship is the engine that drives our relationship with God and with other believers. As we worship God with an undivided heart, we are better able to accomplish God's will in all facets of our lives. Let us take time to examine our heart and give to God the pure worship that He deserves.

Marcia Hare (1798–1870) prayed that she would be released from the bondage of an idol-worshipping heart:

O Lord God Almighty, redeem my soul from its bondage, that I may be free to live hence forth, not for myself; but for you. Help me to put away self, and to remember that this life is not given for my ease, my enjoyment. It is a schooling time for the eternal home you have prepared for those who love you. Keep my eye steadily fixed on that haven of rest and peace, that I may not be faint nor be weary from the length of the way, but may strive to walk worthy of my high calling in all meekness and lowliness of heart. Amen.

I readily take note that what we do on this earth prepares us for eternity. In order for us to think in these terms requires us to have a tender heart, not a stony one. In Ezekiel 11:20, the writer repeats what God told him about why His people were to have a new heart: "That they may walk in My statutes and keep My ordinances and do them. Then they will be My people, and I shall be their God." If people find it difficult to follow God's ordinances today, maybe it's because they still have hearts of stone; they need heart operations that will turn their stones to flesh.

❋ Prayer ❋

Father God, I humbly bow down before You in worship. Tear down all the idols of my life and give me a tender heart that's 100-percent devoted to You. Teach me to obey Your commands as Your child. Amen.

❄ HEART ACTION ❄

Engage in worship. Let go of expectations or worries and allow your heart to be softened so you can praise God and take in His love and strength.

Tea's proper use is to amuse the idle,
and relax the studious, and dilute the
full meals of those who cannot use exercise,
and will not use abstinence.

SAMUEL JOHNSON

EMILIE'S CLASSIC SCONES

- 2 cups flour
- 1 tablespoon baking powder
- 2 tablespoons sugar
- ½ teaspoon salt
- 6 tablespoons butter
- ½ cup buttermilk (or you can use regular milk)
- 1 egg, lightly beaten

Mix dry ingredients. Cut in butter until mixture resembles coarse cornmeal. Make a well in the center and pour in buttermilk or regular milk. Mix until dough clings together and is a bit sticky—don't overmix. Turn out dough onto a floured surface and shape into a 6- to 8-inch round about 1½ inches thick. Quickly cut into pie wedges or use a large round biscuit cutter to cut circles. (The secret of tender scones is a minimum of handling.) Place on ungreased cookie sheet, being sure sides of scones don't touch each other. Brush with egg for a shiny, beautiful brown scone.

Bake at 425° F for 10 to 20 minutes, or until light brown.

You can add all kinds of extras to scones, depending on your taste. Try the following:

- cut-up apples
- currants
- ginger
- orange
- almond flavoring
- cinnamon
- apricots
- fresh blueberries
- cranberries
- chocolate chips

Be in Love with Prayer

When I awake, I am still with You.

—Psalm 139:18

Isn't it great to know that even though we sleep eight to ten hours, when we awake God is still with us? He hasn't dozed off during the early hours of the morning. I know that when I am the closest to Jesus, my prayers come more easily and more often. During dry seasons of life I have to consciously set a time for prayer—and often it's more out of duty than desire. As I abide with my Savior, I don't have to say, "It is time for me to get to my task and pray." No, I pray when there is a need, regardless of the time of day or night.

These last few years have brought me to God's throne because I want to go there, not because I have fallen back to the law. If you aren't there yet, just wait. The sufferings of life will cause you to drop to your knees in earnest prayer.

Earlier in my Christian walk it was hard to understand the meaning behind 1 Thessalonians 5:17, where it says, "Pray without ceasing." Now I have experienced that in real, living color. I pray literally without ceasing. I pray when I wake, pray at mealtime, pray throughout the day—and I end my day with a prayer of thanksgiving for getting me through the day.

When a friend calls to tell you of a prayer need, you don't say, "I'm sorry, but I don't pray again until I go to bed tonight." Of course you wouldn't say that! In fact, I recommend that you pray with the person who's making the request. That way you are sure to pray for their particulars rather than getting distracted with a busy schedule.

No longer is prayer a burden. It's a privilege to be able to pray, not because of the law, but because of the grace of the cross. Embrace this privilege and make it a regular, important part of each day. Be faithful in prayer so you can know of God's faithfulness.

❀ Prayer ❀

Father God, what a privilege it is to pray without ceasing. You have given me the freedom to honor You in prayer at any time or any situation. May I be known as a person who prays. Amen.

❊ Heart Action ❊

Pray with a friend this week.

I know Christ dwells within me all the time,
guiding me and inspiring me whenever
I do or say anything. A light of which I
caught no glimmer before comes to me at
the very moment when it is needed.

Saint Therese of Lisieux

Give of Yourself

*Give, and it will be given to you. They
will pour into your lap a good measure—
pressed down, shaken together, and running
over. For by your standard of measure
it will be measured to you in return.*

—LUKE 6:38

The world waits until someone gives before giving back; however, Scripture tells us to give first, then it will be added unto us. We can do this with our love, affection, material things; with our friendship, help, and attention. You might have grown up with a limited, conditional kind of giving. If so, it is time for healing. We are so fortunate to have the ultimate example of "giving first" in our Lord. He gave unconditional love, He gave His life, He gives His mercy and grace.

St. Francis of Assisi's words are a great encouragement to live as an instrument of God's giving goodness.

*Lord, make me an instrument of Thy peace;
where there is hatred, let me sow love;*

where there is injury, pardon;
where there is doubt, faith;
where there is despair, hope;
where there is darkness, light;
and where there is sadness, joy.
O Divine Master,
grant that I may not so much seek to be consoled
  as to console;
to be understood, as to understand;
to be loved, as to love;
for it is in giving that we receive,
it is in pardoning that we are pardoned,
and it is in dying that we are born to Eternal
  Life.
Amen.

Become someone who is eager to give freely and to give first. And when others offer you injury or doubt or sorrow, return to them only forgiveness, faith, and joy.

❖ Prayer ❖

Father God, You are truly a God of
giving. Thank You so much for all You
have given me. I can never repay You
for all Your graciousness. Amen.

❃ HEART ACTION ❃

Are you waiting for someone to give to you before you are willing to give to him or her? Try the reverse: Give to that person first. Step out today in faith and give.

Conduct is what we do; character is what we are. Conduct is the outward life; character is the life unseen, hidden within, yet evidenced by that which is seen... Character is the state of the heart; conduct is its outward expression. Character is the root of the tree, conduct, the fruit it bears.

E.M. BOUNDS

Is Your Glass Half-Full?

God saw all that He had made,
and behold, it was very good.
And there was evening and there
was morning, the sixth day.

—Genesis 1:31

As we look at life, are we bound to the idea that bad things happen to people? Look at all the bad news on television and radio. The newspapers are full of disasters: people dying of illness, accidents, drownings, fires destroying property, uprisings in countries abroad, and on and on. Do you sometimes ask God, "Why me?"

As we look around, we get the idea that everything is falling apart, and our whole world is in a spiral downward. Charles L. Allen expressed this idea about our perspective: Our glasses aren't half-empty; they are really half-full. He says,

It seems to be a general belief that the will of God is to make things distasteful for us, like taking medicine when we are sick or going to the dentist. Somebody needs to tell us that sunrise is also God's will. In fact, the good things in life far outweigh the bad. There are more sunrises than cyclones.

His glass was certainly half-full.

There's a story of a young boy who was on top of a pile of horse manure digging as fast and as hard as he could. His father, seeing his son work so hard on a pile of smelly waste, asked, "Weston, what are you doing on that pile of horse manure?" Weston replied, "Daddy, with this much horse manure there must be a pony here somewhere." This son certainly had his glass half-full. You, too, can choose to be positive in all events of life. There is goodness in everything—if we will only look for it.

❊ PRAYER ❊

Father God, thank You for helping me be a positive person. I appreciate You giving me the ability to be an encourager to those around me. It certainly makes life so much more exciting. Amen.

❊ HEART ACTION ❊

Take any situation that comes and find the goodness in it. Look at a trial as a chance to draw closer to God. Look at a struggling relationship as a chance to be faithful and forgiving. Then look at the sunset and praise God for the beauty He made, which is, for us, a constant reminder of His love and presence.

Tea is wealth itself,
Because there is nothing that cannot be lost,
No problem that will not disappear,
No burden that will not float away,
Between the first sip and the last.

THE MINISTER OF LEAVES

The Spirit of Tea

Now stir the fire, and close the shutters fast,
Let fall the curtains, wheel the sofa round,
And, while the bubbling and loud hissing urn
Throws up a steamy column and the cups
That cheer but not inebriate, wait on each,
So let us welcome peaceful ev'ning in.

WILLIAM COWPER

Perhaps the idea of a tea party takes you back to childhood. Do you remember dressing up and putting on your best manners as you sipped pretend tea out of tiny cups and shared pretend delicacies with your friends, your parents, or your teddy bears? Were you lucky enough to know adults who cared enough to share tea parties with you? And are you lucky enough to have a little person with whom you could share a tea party today? Is there a little girl inside you who longs for a lovely time of childish imagination and "so big" manners?

It could be that the mention of teatime brings quieter memories—cups of amber liquid sipped in peaceful solitude on a big porch, or friendly confidences shared over steaming cups. So many of my own special times of closeness—with my husband, my children, my friends—have begun with putting a kettle on to boil and pulling out a tea tray.

But even if you don't care for tea—if you prefer coffee or cocoa or lemonade or ice water, or if you like chunky mugs better than gleaming silver or delicate china, or if you find the idea of traditional tea too formal and a bit intimidating—there's still room for you at the tea table, and I think you would love it there! I have shared tea with so many people—from business executives to book-club ladies to five-year-old boys. And I have found that few can resist a tea party when it is served with the right spirit.

You see, it's not tea itself that speaks to the soul with such a satisfying message—although I must confess that I adore the warmth and fragrance of a cup of Earl Grey or Red Zinger. And it's not the teacups themselves that bring such a message of beauty and serenity and friendship—although my teacups do bring much pleasure.

It's not the tea, in other words, that makes teatime special, it's the spirit of the tea party.

It's what happens when women or men or children make a place in their life for the rituals of sharing. It's what happens when we bother with the little extras that feed the soul and nurture the senses and make space for unhurried conversation. And when that happens, it doesn't really matter what fills the cups or holds the liquid.

It really isn't the tea.

It's the spirit of the tea party.

And it is in that spirit I hope you will join me.

❖ PRAYER ❖

God, grant me a giving heart that wishes to share the treasures of tea and hospitality and kindness. Remind me to bother with those extras that make the difference in the lives of family members, friends, and strangers. Amen.

❖ HEART ACTION ❖

Ask another to join you for a time of tea and conversation and connection.

If I am inconsiderate about the comfort of others, or their feelings, or even their little weaknesses; if I am careless about their little hurts and miss opportunities to smooth their way; if I make the sweet running of

household wheels more difficult to accomplish,
then I know nothing of Calvary's love.

AMY CARMICHAEL

❊ THE TEAPOT MAKER'S MARK ❊

To learn where, when, and by whom a piece was made, look for the maker's mark on the bottom. The pattern name and/or number may be included, as might be the name, initials, or special mark of the designer or artist. Though not always complete, this capsule history provides the simple facts of a teapot's origin.

What strong medicinal, but rich, scents
from the decaying leaves! The rain falling
on the freshly dried herbs and leaves, and
filling the pools and ditches into which they
have dropped thus clean and rigid, will soon
convert them into tea,—green, black, brown,
and yellow teas, of all degrees of strength,
enough to set all Nature a-gossiping.

HENRY DAVID THOREAU

❖ ETIQUETTE FOR THE GUEST ❖

Important things to remember as a guest:

- Be punctual, but not early.
- Cancel only if there is an emergency.
- Offer to help the hostess if help is needed.
- Be a good mixer with the other guests.
- If there is a theme to the tea, dress according to the theme. It will add a special touch to the event.
- Even though you enjoy talking, try not to be the last to leave.
- Be sure to say a goodbye to the hostess.
- Write a thank-you note within 24 hours of the party.

Live Each Day to Its Fullest

*Always giving thanks for all things
in the name of our Lord Jesus Christ
to God, even the Father.*

—Ephesians 5:20

During my season of illness, I spent a lot of time waiting in the reception areas of doctors' offices. (In most cases the wait lasted at least an hour beyond the time my appointment was scheduled.) During this time I had the opportunity to talk to people who had been diagnosed with a disease that would shorten their life expectancy—in a word, they have received "bad news." Through this, I became aware that I no longer wanted to wait for bad news before I began to appreciate life. I had always been a thankful person, filled with gratitude to God for what He had given me. But now I'm even more careful not to take one single day for granted, because I understand that life can be very short. I don't want to postpone one day of thankfulness for the life I have; it is so precious.

Our situation can change at the drop of a hat. Bad

news can come in a moment. We have no promise that we will live forever—in fact, "it is appointed for men to die" (Hebrews 9:27). As I look around today, I can truly thank God abundantly for the simple things of life: sleep, walking, running, heartbeats, husband, children, grandchildren, peace, and so on. Things I used to take for granted. But now I never want to give into the fear of what might come next, a fear of the unknown. I want to be grateful to God for all He gives to me and my family. Several times a day I find myself taking moments to thank God for all my blessings. I don't want to leave out the most minute reason for appreciation.

I think that time of uncertainty was a wonderful experience for me, because it has made me appreciate what I have. I'm far more aware of how bountiful my life is and has been. I truly have a thankful heart because of that season in my life. Today the glass is truly half-full and not half-empty.

❧ PRAYER ❧

Father God, give me eyes to see and ears to hear all the good news in my life. There is so much to be grateful for each day. When I receive bad news, let me turn to You for Your peace and direction. Give me the desire to

laugh and love and praise even when times
are tough. Your love and grace carry me to
a deep sense of joy that can remain during
times of perseverance or doubt. Amen.

❉ HEART ACTION ❉

Gratitude will override your deepest fears. Spend time reflecting on all that you are grateful for right now. You don't know what tomorrow will bring, but you can say "thank You" today to the Lord.

Tomato Basil Sandwiches

- ½ cup unsalted butter, cut up
- 1 teaspoon tomato puree
- ¼ teaspoon sugar
- ¼ teaspoon salt
- ⅛ teaspoon pepper
- ¼ teaspoon lemon juice
- ¼ cup lightly packed chopped fresh basil or 1 tablespoon dried fresh basil
- 1 pound fresh tomatoes
- 8 slices white bread, crusts removed
- 8 slices whole wheat bread, crusts removed
- salt and freshly ground pepper to taste

To make basil butter, combine butter, tomato puree, sugar, salt, pepper, and lemon juice in a food processor. Process until blended. Add basil leaves. Pulse with on/off turns until blended. Set aside at room temperature. To make the filling, use a small knife to cut a small cross in bottom skin of each tomato. Place tomatoes into boiling water for 20 seconds.

Cool in cold water. Drain. Peel, core, and seed tomatoes. Chop tomato flesh very fine. Stir gently in strainer to drain. Just before serving, spread one side of each slice of bread with basil butter. Spread tomato filling on each slice. Season with salt and pepper to taste. Cut each sandwich in half. Serve fresh. Makes 16.

❄ ❄ ❄

Though we eat little flesh and drink no wine,
Yet let's be merry; we'll have tea and toast;
Custards for supper, and an endless host
Of syllabubs and jellies and mince-pies,
And other such ladylike luxuries.

—PERCY BYSSHE SHELLEY

A Life of Blessings

*Blessed are the peacemakers, for they
shall be called sons of God.*

—Matthew 5:9

History is full of people who have been peace-makers. They have been willing to risk their well-being, health, and wealth to stand in the gap between separated parties to help heal disagreements and avoid wars. Even within families we can witness the terrible destruction that takes place between warring members. Sometimes the road seems to be strewn with fragmented lives. But Jesus is quite clear that He wants *all* of His children to be known as peacemakers. Scripture makes it plain that we are to be known as ambassadors of peace toward…

- *God:* "God has given us the task of reconciling people to him" (2 Corinthians 5:18 NLT).
- *Ourselves:* "Joy fills hearts that are planning peace!" (Proverbs 12:20 NLT).
- *Others:* "Those who are peacemakers will plant

seeds of peace and reap a harvest of righteousness" (James 3:18 NLT).

Since the blessing of being a peacemaker is to be called a child of God, we can experience the joy of goodness, happiness, and peace within our own lives. When we exhibit these positive traits we will begin to reflect...

- *Contentment with ourselves:* We will know who we are in Christ, thus giving us the contentment we have long searched for.
- *Optimism in our faith:* We will exhibit a love for God and reflect a positive faith in how we look at life and the events that come our way.
- *Relational connectedness:* We will have deeper friendships. People will be bonded closer to us. We will become better friends.
- *Mercy:* We will be more willing and capable to give mercy in our dealings with ourselves and others.
- *Doing what is right:* We will have a benchmark to judge proper behavior for ourselves.

Make Jesus Christ your Savior and become a peacemaker.

❋ PRAYER ❋

Father God, may I have the courage to step
out and become a peacemaker. Let it start
with me and ripple out to others I meet.
Help me humble myself so I can be lifted
up and used for Your kingdom. Amen.

❋ HEART ACTION ❋

Bury the hatchet that causes war within yourself
and with others. Take your sins to the cross and leave
them there, never to pick them up again.

Interview Your Friends

A man of too many friends comes to ruin, but there is a friend who sticks closer than a brother.

—Proverbs 18:24

A good paraphrase of this opening Scripture is, "A woman of too many friends will be broken in pieces." Indiscriminately chosen friends may bring trouble, but a genuine friend sticks with you through thick and thin.

Our friends have a positive or negative effect upon our lives. Many of us have told our children to be careful who they run with because people are known by the company they keep. There are certain areas in our lives where we have no choice about who we are around, such as work, church, neighbors, and social clubs. In these settings we are thrown together. However, in our family and private times we can be very discriminating about those with whom we associate. We must realize that our time and energy are among our most precious assets. Therefore it's important to make wise choices in the selection of people we will spend time with. Are they people who build us up and encourage us to be better people than we would be by ourselves?

Why have you chosen the people who are closest to you? How do they contribute to who you are? It's not that you cast off those who don't contribute positively to your life, but I encourage you to reevaluate your relationships and see how you respond when you are around certain people. Do you respect them? Do they encourage you to grow? Do you have a kindred spirit? Do you share like values? If you can't answer in the affirmative, you might want to review how much time you spend with these people. Some changes might be in order.

You have a limited amount of time to spend with others, so select wisely; much of who you are—positive as well as negative—will be formed by the friends you keep.

❋ Prayer ❋

Lord, draw me close to others who love You and who want a deeper relationship with You. Help me to choose friends wisely so that I am supported in the things that matter most to me, like faith and family. Also, give me a heart to be a positive influence on others. Remind

me to turn my thoughts to You and Your love
when my attitude becomes negative. Amen.

❋ HEART ACTION ❋

Make a date with a friend you are missing. Don't worry that a long time has passed since you last spoke. Start with where you are right now and let her know that you miss her and her presence in your life.

The spirit of the tea beverage is one of
peace, comfort, and refinement.

ARTHUR GRAY

Say "Yes" for Tomorrow

Rejoice that your names are recorded in heaven.

—Luke 10:20

A few days after Roy Rogers passed away at his home in Apple Valley, California, a local Christian television station broadcast a tribute to his life. In one of the segments, Dale Evans, Roy's wife, sang a song entitled, "Say 'Yes' for Tomorrow." This song was dedicated to the memory of Roy's early decision to put his trust in Jesus as his Savior.

While listening to this song I began to think back over my own life, back to when I invited Jesus, as my Lord, into my heart. At that time I made the most important decision in my life. I truly said "'yes' for tomorrow," in that I settled my eternity by saying "yes" to Jesus. I was a teenager who came from a Jewish background. Even though my decision for Christ didn't set well with my extended family of aunts and uncles, it did settle for me what my tomorrows would be. My direction for the future was decided. As I've matured in my life I've realized that many adults have never made that affirmation.

What a shame to search all one's life and then, at the end of life, be unsure what the future might hold.

Dale Evans shared with her audience that Roy had made this decision a long time ago. And since she also was a believer she had the assurance that she would be reunited with Roy in heaven.

If you haven't settled what tomorrow will be, take time today to guarantee your destination. Confirm to your family that you will be united together forever in heaven.

❖ PRAYER ❖

Father God, I thank You for providing a way so I can know where my tomorrow will be. Thank You for sending Jesus to pay the price on the cross for my sins. I'm so glad I said "Yes" as a young girl! Amen.

❖ HEART ACTION ❖

If you haven't answered the tomorrow question, today might be the day to settle the most important question in your life.

❀ PERSONALIZED TEA PARTY ❀

In advance of a tea party, create a list of what makes each woman you have invited beautiful in your eyes. Use examples from that woman's life of how she demonstrates areas of beauty and grace. Share these with the group and encourage others to offer their words of honor as you lift up each person in attendance.

Where there's tea there's hope.

SIR ARTHUR PINERO

It's Okay to Be Selfish

You shall love your neighbor as yourself.

—LEVITICUS 19:18

Yes, I give you permission to be selfish at times. One thing I notice about so many people is that they are burned out because they spend so much time serving others that they have no time for themselves. As a young mom I was going from sunup to late in the evening just doing the things that moms do. When evening came around I was exhausted. All I wanted to do was take a hot bath and slip into bed and catch as much sleep as possible before I was awakened in the night by one of the children.

After several years I remember saying to myself, *I've got to have some time just for me—I need help.* One of the things I did was to get up a half hour before everyone else so I could spend time in the Scriptures over an early cup of tea. This one activity had an incredibly positive effect upon my outlook. I went on to making arrangements to get my hair and nails taken care of periodically. I was even known to purchase a new outfit (on sale of course) occasionally. As I matured I discovered that I became a better parent and wife when I had time for myself and my emotional tank was filled up. I soon realized I had plenty left over to share with my loved ones.

When you're able to spend some time just for you, you will be more relaxed, and your family and home will function better. I find these to be beneficial time-outs:

- taking a warm bath by candlelight
- getting a massage
- having my hair and nails done
- meeting a friend for lunch
- listening to my favorite CD
- reading a good book
- writing a poem
- watching a classic movie

Sometimes quick experiences pay big dividends. You need refreshment and renewal. Don't let yourself become so overwhelmed by your responsibilities that you forget how to nourish yourself with those things that give you a lift…like a cup of tea, perhaps?

❊ PRAYER ❊

*Lord, help my spirit to be still and silent
before You. I pray that I will carve out time
to be with You and enjoy simple pleasures
that fill me with happiness and hope and
peace. It is good to take time for myself and
to nurture my life. I want to give and give to
my family, my job, and to You...guide me
toward balance. Lead me to the joy of quiet
time and "me" time so I am refreshed and even
more prepared to serve and to love. Amen.*

❊ HEART ACTION ❊

Select a way to relax and restore yourself today.
Choose an inspiring verse from Scripture and meditate on it while you relax. Your outlook will change
dramatically.

Lift Yourself Up

*You formed my inward parts; You
wove me in my mother's womb...I am
fearfully and wonderfully made.*

—Psalm 139:13-14

*If I could only have a straight nose, a tummy tuck,
blonde hair, larger (or smaller) breasts, or be more
like so-and-so, I would be okay as a person.* Never have
I heard women satisfied with how God made them.

"God must have made a mistake when He made
me." "I'm certainly the exception to His model creation." "There's so much wrong with me, I'm just
paralyzed over who I am."

These negative thoughts poison our system. We
can't be lifted up when we spend so much time tear-
ing ourselves down. When we are in a negative mode,
we can always find verification for what we're looking
for. If we concentrate on the negative, we lose sight
of all the positive aspects of our lives. We can always
justify our damaging assumptions when we overlook
the good God has for us.

These critical vibes create more negative vibes.

Soon we are in a downward spiral. When you concentrate on your imperfections you have a tendency to look at what's wrong and not what's right. Putting yourself down can have some severe personal consequences.

Have you ever realized that God made you uniquely different from everyone else? (Even if you're a twin you are different.) Yes, it is important to work on improving your imperfections—but don't dwell on them so much that you forget who you are in the sight of God. The more positive you are toward yourself the more you will grow into the person God had in mind for you when you were created. Go easy on yourself. None of us will ever be perfect. The only way we will improve our self-image is by being positive and acknowledging that we are God's creation. Negativity tears down; positivity builds up.

❋ Prayer ❋

Father God, You knew me while I was in my mother's womb. I hunger to be the woman You created me to be. Help me become all that You had in mind when You made me. Cut off all my negative thoughts and expressions. I want others around me to know me as a positive person. I want to reflect Your love. Amen.

❄ HEART ACTION ❄

Build up the courage of others, and also tend to how you treat yourself. You are loved by a mighty God. You were made in His image, and you have value beyond measure. Let go of goals for perfection so you can appreciate your strengths, abilities, and unique wonders.

*Nobody can teach you
how to make the perfect cup of tea.
It just happens over time.*

JILL DUPLEIX

TANGERINE TEA

- 7 to 8 teaspoons of orange pekoe tea leaves
- 8 cups boiling water
- 2 tangerines, cleaned, cut into ¼-inch to ½-inch slices
- whole cloves

Warm teapot with hot water, empty it, and dry it off. Add tea leaves to pot. Pour boiling water over leaves and let it steep for 5 minutes. Use a tea cozy to retain heat. Cut tangerine slices in half, stick a few cloves in the rind of the tangerine skins, and place two half slices in each teacup before pouring strained tea. Sweeten with honey or sugar if desired.

Be an Example

...Proving to be examples to the flock.

—1 Peter 5:3

Over and over I have attempted to be an example by doing rather than telling. I feel that God's great truths are "caught" and not always "taught." In the book of Deuteronomy, Moses (the author) says the following about God's commandments, statutes, and judgments: "You shall teach them diligently to your sons and shall talk of them when you sit in your house and when you walk by the way and when you lie down and when you rise up" (6:7). In other words, at all times we are to be examples.

It is amazing how much we can teach by example in every situation: at home, at the beach, while jogging, when resting, when eating—in every part of the day. It's amazing how often I catch our children and grandchildren imitating the values we exhibited in our home—something as little as a lighted candle to warm the heart, to a thank-you when food is being served in a restaurant.

Little eyes are peering around to see how we

behave when we think no one is looking. Are we consistent with what we say we believe? If we talk calmness and patience, how do we respond when standing in a slow line at the market? How does our conversation go when there is a slowdown on Friday evening's freeway drive? Do we go by the rules on the freeway (having two people or more in the car while driving in the carpool lane, going the speed limit, and obeying all traffic signs)?

How can we show God's love? By helping people out when they are in need of assistance, even when it is not convenient. We can be good neighbors. Sending out thank-you cards after receiving a gift shows our appreciation for the gift and the person. Being kind to animals and the environment when we go to the park for a campout or picnic shows good stewardship. We are continually setting some kind of example whether we know it or not.

❄ PRAYER ❄

Father God, let my life be an example to those around me, especially the little ones who are learning the ways of faith. May I exhibit proper conduct even when no one is around. I want to be obedient to Your guiding principles. Thank You for Your example. Amen.

❧ Heart Action ❧

Do you practice what you preach? Become aware of the times when you are not living out the principles and kindnesses that you hold dear. Find fresh ways to show God's love and express your gifts and your compassion.

Cambric tea was hot water and milk, with only a taste of tea in it, but little girls felt grown-up when their mothers let them drink cambric tea.

Laura Ingalls Wilder

The Wise Are Mature

We are no longer to be children, tossed here
and there by waves and carried about by every
wind of doctrine, by the trickery
of men, by craftiness in deceitful scheming;
but speaking the truth in love, we are
to grow up in all aspects into Him.

—Ephesians 4:14-15

God does not want us to remain spiritually immature. Many of the 30-to-40-year-old women I meet seem to dwell on how old they are. There doesn't seem to be much hope or time for them to make an impact in life. I always reassure them how beautiful the older decades are. Each season of life has so much to offer. Life becomes richer the more mature we become. Benjamin Jowett once wrote,

> Though I am growing old, I maintain that the best part is yet to come—the time when one may see things more dispassionately and know oneself and others more truly, and perhaps be able to do more, and in religion rest centered in

a few simple truths. I do not want to ignore the other side, that one will not be able to see so well or walk so far or read so much. But there may be more peace within, more communications with God, more real light instead of distraction about many things, better relations with others, and fewer mistakes.

In our Christian walk we are encouraged not to remain like babes and children, but to wean ourselves from spiritual milk and soft food and grow into healthier foods. God wants us to exhibit signs of maturity, and many times this comes through very difficult life situations. My experience validates that we grow through difficulties and not through just the good times.

If we are not mature, the reason is observable: We have not been workers but idlers in our study of the Bible. Those who are just "Sunday Christians" will never grow to maturity—it takes the study of the Scriptures to become meat-eaters of God's Word. We must be workers in the Scriptures. Paul told Timothy, "Be diligent to present yourself approved to God as a workman...accurately handling the word of truth" (2 Timothy 2:15). We must roll up our sleeves and do the job ourselves instead of expecting a pastor or teacher to do it for us.

❊ Prayer ❊

Father God, thank You for inspiring men of old to write Your Scriptures. They have become my Scriptures; they have become my salvation. Without the knowledge of Scripture my life would be tossed about like the waves in the wind. Thank You for my stability. Amen.

❊ Heart Action ❊

Discover God's strength and comfort by reading His Word each day. Single out a phrase or even a word that really speaks to your heart and carry that with you during your day.

It's Okay to Disagree

Make my joy complete by being of the
same mind, maintaining the same love,
united in spirit, intent on one purpose.

—Philippians 2:2

For many years I thought a couple was never to disagree—that Bob and I, as a couple, should agree at all times. Then I began to realize that this wasn't always possible because Bob and I came from different backgrounds.

We can justify why we think a certain way because of the way we were raised. The problem with this is we both can justify our choices equally well. Everyone tends to believe that the others in their lives should think like they do. But if this isn't true in real life, how can we always agree? Also, as I studied the basic temperament types, I soon realized that my Bob had a different temperament than I did. This means we tend to respond differently to situations or ideas.

With this new data, Bob and I gave each other

permission to disagree. We became better listeners and weren't so defensive and argumentative. With our new knowledge, we weren't as easily frustrated just because we didn't think alike. It was okay—we agreed we were able to disagree. What a freeing experience! With this agreement we seemed to respect each other's diversity of opinion more. I had a more loving attitude toward Bob because he looked at me in a different way—my ideas and concerns were more important to him.

Everyone wins in this outlook. Because of this arrangement, Bob and I are much more able to be united in one mind, one love, one spirit, and one purpose. To this day we are strongly committed to the real issues of life. In the big issues we are as one; in the lesser issues we still differ—and that's what makes marriage so much fun.

❈ PRAYER ❈

Father God, help me and my husband have the flexibility to agree to disagree. What a difference it will make in our marriage. Show me how I can have a greater tolerance for our differences and still be able to agree on the big issues of life. Thank You for making each of us unique and special. Amen.

❄ HEART ACTION ❄

Be willing to listen to the thoughts and expressions of the people in your life. Be open to them even when they disagree. And when you disagree with them…approach them with respect and friendship.

There is no trouble so great or grave
that cannot be much diminished
by a nice cup of tea.

BERNARD-PAUL HEROUX

The Blessing of Tea

There are few hours in life more
agreeable than the hour dedicated to the
ceremony known as afternoon tea.

HENRY JAMES

If you really want to, you can grab a quick cup of tea.

You can drive by the fast-food window and collect a foam cup full of hot water with a little plastic lid, a packet of sweetener, and a teabag. Then you can sit there in the drive-through lane (while cars honk behind you), lift the lid, stick in the little gauze bag, and set your tea in the cup holder to steep while you steer back out into traffic.

Or if you're in a hurry at home or at the office, you can always heat a mug of water in the microwave. Then you can plunk in your teabag or stir in some spiced-tea mix and carry the whole thing back to your desk to gulp while you work.

You really can do that if you prefer.

But I hope you won't do it.

You see, if you insist on instant, you'll get your tea, but you'll miss one of tea's most beautiful benefits—the blessing of slowing down to enjoy it. You'll be having your tea but losing the opportunity to stake out an island of calm serenity in the chaotic ocean of daily life.

Whether your teatime is simple or elaborate, a solitary moment or a friendly gathering, it can help you make room for stillness in even the most frantic day. As a result, its potential for stress reduction is enormous.

Tea takes time—and that's part of the magic. You can't hurry it without losing something vital. The act of making and drinking tea forces us to slow down—and I truly believe our bodies and spirits are desperate to slow down from the frantic pace our culture sets for us today.

People in our society don't like to wait, but you simply cannot hurry a good pot of tea.

You put on the kettle, then you must wait for the water to boil. And while you're waiting, there are little things to attend to. You rinse out the teapot. You fill the cream pitcher and the sugar bowl and set out the teacup—the prettiest one you have. You might pick a flower or set a candle in its holder or rummage through the cabinet for a pretty plate. Even if you haven't had time to bake, you open a package of cookies and arrange them on the plate.

No, none of these things are absolutely necessary. You can always go back to microwaving water and fishing your cookie directly from the package. You can drink your tea standing up at the counter or gulp it as you run out the door. But again, you'll be missing the opportunity.

You see, boiling the water in a kettle is part of the ritual. Arranging the tea tray is part of the ritual. Preparing and enjoying tea is a ritual in itself.

I love what my friend Yoli Brogger calls it: "a ceremony of loveliness." And I believe with all my heart that human beings crave ritual and ceremony (and loveliness) in our lives.

When we do things a certain way, the way we have done them in the past, the way others before us have done them, something deep in our spirits is comforted.

Children instinctively know this; that's why they delight in family traditions. Teenagers may rebel against established customs, but they create their own. (Watch a teenager get ready to go out in the evening and you know how important ritual is to him or her.) Most of us, as we grow older, also grow to cherish the rituals of our lives.

Enrich your life with the blessings that tea brings to your life: service, hospitality, generosity, ritual, sharing, tradition, comfort, and so much more.

❀ PRAYER ❀

Father God, let one of my most important rituals be to give thanks to You in all things. I want to share this practice with others as I live gratitude out in my words and actions. Amen.

❀ HEART ACTION ❀

Start a few simple traditions or rituals that illuminate faith and hope. Invite your family and friends and others to join in these traditions.

It takes so little to make us glad,
Just a cheering clasp of a friendly hand,
Just a word from one who can understand;
And we finish the task we long had planned,
And we lose the doubt and the fear we had—
So little it takes to make us glad.

—IDA GOLDSMITH MORRIS

❋ Finishing Touches ❋

Adorn your cake or other goodies like cupcakes, cookies, or salads with edible flowers. Here is a list of some of the most popular edible flowers and their flavors. Be sure to research any others you choose before placing them on food items.

- nasturtium—spicy
- chives—onion flavor
- squash, daylily—like a vegetable
- calendula—buttery
- mint, pansy—minty
- sage, marigold—herbal
- rose, violet—floral

Leave a Legacy

I am mindful of the sincere faith within you, which first dwelt in your grandmother Lois and your mother Eunice, and I am sure that it is in you as well.

—2 TIMOTHY 1:5

Have you ever been challenged regarding what kind of legacy you are going to leave to your heirs? We all leave behind us some type of belief system, regardless of how we live our lives. It will either be good and positive or it will be bad and negative. Our heirs will reflect what kind of influence we had on their lives.

Paul writes this second letter to his friend Timothy and challenges him to remember the influence his mother and grandmother had upon his life. In 2 Timothy 1:3-18, Paul encourages Timothy to concentrate on the past, present, and future aspects of developing a legacy. Paul wants Timothy to "fan the flame" of his faith for God. The character development Timothy needed was to embrace and live out the fact that God had not given him a spirit of timidity (cowardice) but one of power, love, and discipline.

The second part of the legacy was to follow the plan that God had given. Paul warned Timothy that at times he might have to suffer for preaching the gospel. He stressed that Timothy was not to be ashamed, but believe and be convinced that Jesus is able to guard what has been entrusted to Him.

Another aspect of passing this legacy to others is to pattern our lives from what we have seen. Paul stressed that we retain the standard of sound words we have heard from him. We are to guard, through the Holy Spirit, the treasure (gospel) that has been entrusted to us.

The last aspect of developing a worthwhile legacy is to pass it on. Paul told Timothy to entrust these truths to "faithful men who will be able to teach others also" (2 Timothy 2:1-2). Be a mom who cares about the kind of legacy you leave when the Lord calls you home. Teach your children these truths:

- Fan the flame of passion for God
- Follow God's plan for you
- Pattern your life from what you've learned
- Pass it on to those who will follow

Investing in the faith of the next generation is one of the most important things you can do. Be a teacher, a mentor, a godly parent, a caring neighbor, and a follower of Jesus. Your legacy will be the love and truth of Christ.

❊ PRAYER ❊

Lord, give me a heart for my children and the children of others. When I am nervous about teaching or instructing, give me the strength and confidence in You that I need to be obedient to Your will. I want my legacy to be a reflection of Your grace and goodness. Amen.

❊ HEART ACTION ❊

Share your legacy of faith and belief and hope with the people you care about most.

Think Positively

Whatever is true, whatever is honorable,
whatever is right, whatever is pure, whatever
is lovely, whatever is of good repute, if
there is any excellence and if anything
worthy of praise, dwell on these things.

—Philippians 4:8

An old Chinese proverb states, "What we think, we are." That is so true. Our thought processes determine who we are. If we think lustful thoughts, we become lustful. If thoughts of anger enter our minds, we become angry. What we think is what we begin to feel. Anger, stress, lust, bitterness, and unhappiness have a way of weaseling into our minds and creating a pattern of negativity. We increase our stress and frustration with life when we constantly dialog with ourselves, muttering, "I hate my job." "I don't like Mary." "This place is always a mess." "I hate being married." "No one ever helps me with the chores." "This job is lousy."

If we continue in this mental conversation, we'll begin to internalize these negative beliefs, which is very destructive to our lives.

In order to nip these attacks in the bud, we have to pursue the thoughts described in today's passage. We must be willing to choose which road we will travel—one that spirals downward or one that spirals upward into a more healthy environment. Paul tells us to think on things that are...

- honorable
- right
- pure
- lovely
- of good repute
- excellent and worthy of praise

This is certainly contrary to what the world, with its immorality, tells us to do. We must make a conscious effort to think in these godly terms. When we do, our whole world will change. These thoughts will give us new criteria for what we read, view, listen, eat, and think. We will find great riches, and the stresses of life will be much reduced.

❋ PRAYER ❋

Father God, You have given me only one life to live, and I certainly want it to reflect

*my love for You. Give me the strength to
make the proper choices for my mind, body,
and soul. I do want to travel the road less
traveled—the road to You. Amen.*

❈ HEART ACTION ❈

Fill your heart and life with good words and ideas
and with righteous ideas and hopeful dreams.

*Spread love everywhere you go: First of all in
your own house…let no one ever come to you
without leaving better and happier. Be the
living expression of God's kindness: kindness
in your face, kindness in your eyes, kindness in
your smile, kindness in your warm greeting.*

MOTHER TERESA

Chocolate Scones

- 2½ cups all-purpose flour
- ½ cup unsweetened cocoa powder
- ½ cup sugar
- 2 teaspoons baking powder
- ½ teaspoon salt
- ½ cup (1 stick) chilled unsalted butter, cut into ½-inch cubes
- 1¼ cups chilled whipping cream
- 1 large egg yolk
- whole milk

Preheat oven to 425° F. Whisk flour, cocoa powder, sugar, baking powder, and salt in large bowl to blend. Rub in butter with fingertips until coarse meal forms. Whisk cream and egg yolk in a small bowl to blend. Stir cream mixture into flour mixture just to blend. Transfer to lightly floured surface. Knead dough gently 5 times to bring it together. Using palms, pat dough out into a ¾-inch-thick round. Using 2½-inch round biscuit cutter, cut out scones. Gather scraps, pat dough out, and cut out additional scones. Transfer scones to a large baking sheet. Brush tops lightly with milk. Bake scones until puffed and dry around edges, about 18 minutes at 425° F. Transfer baked scones to wire rack to cool slightly. Bake ahead of time. Makes about 18.

Serve warm or at room temperature with jam and clotted cream or mock Devonshire cream.

MOCK DEVONSHIRE CREAM

- ½ cup heavy cream or 8 ounces softened cream cheese
- 2 tablespoons confectioner's sugar
- ½ cup sour cream

In a chilled bowl, beat cream until medium-stiff peaks form, adding sugar during the last few minutes of beating. (If you are using cream cheese, just stir together with sugar.) Fold in sour cream and blend. Makes 1½ cups.

Treasure Life

I came that they may have life,
and have it abundantly.

—JOHN 10:10

During my lengthy bout with sickness I again renewed my zeal to treasure life. I recall that as I sat in the doctor's office to receive my chemotherapy treatment every 21 days, I saw so many people—some young, some old—who were gravely ill with various forms of cancer. As I left after my two-and-a-half hour treatment I was able to truly be grateful for my life. Now, each morning as I wake there is a new freshness to the day, and each evening as I put my head on the pillow I am so grateful to God for His goodness to me.

Some time ago my daughter, Jenny, shared with me something I wasn't even aware of. She stated, "Mom, you and Dad have always used the phrase 'How blessed and thankful we are for where we are in life.' But Mom, it wasn't always good news. Yet you both have been so great about saying how well God provides. In the future my own family is going to say *blessed* and *thankful* more often. Thanks, Mom, for showing me how to have more gratitude." What a joy to receive such a comment from my daughter!

I truly believe we are to treasure life to the fullest. Too often we take this incredible gift of life too much for granted. Appreciation for everything—minor and major events—puts things in perspective and allows us to live a more abundant life. When we feel grateful it affects our whole being. All the trivial issues seem to fall away—and I've discovered that often there's a laugh at the end of the rain.

❀ Prayer ❀

Lord, may every step I take today lead me closer to a heart of gratitude. I want to notice the beauty in nature that surrounds me. I want my heart to be glad each time I see the faces of my children and my family. I want compassion to overflow each moment I am in the presence of need or pain. Help me to taste the sweetness of life by living it fully, abundantly, and gratefully. Amen.

❀ Heart Action ❀

Rejoice in today. Whatever you are dealing with or anticipating or regretting, that is not meant for this time of thanksgiving. Be grateful even in the trials. Each obstacle you face presents you with an opportunity to lean on the Lord.

I shall not pass this way again;
Then let me now relieve some pain,
Remove some barrier from the road,
Or brighten some one's heavy load.

EVA ROSE YORK

Let Your Child Be Your Teacher

Children are a gift of the LORD, the fruit of the womb is a reward.

—Psalm 127:3

We so often think that we are to be our children's teachers, but in reality they can also be our teachers. As our children respond to us in verbal as well as nonverbal fashion, they often are not very kind with their rebuttals. Often as we walk away from an encounter (no matter what age our children are), we feel less confident and more vulnerable than we did before. My children taught me much about patience, how to handle confrontation, unconditional love, respect, problem solving, rejection, and the ever-changing aspects of life.

Amid your child-rearing frustrations, take on the attitude that your children are actually teaching you some very valuable facets of character development. Rather than becoming upset with their uncooperative behavior, ask God, "What are You trying to teach me in this situation?" Take these opportunities to discover important insights into life. When you begin to look upon your children as your teachers, you won't become nearly as irritated by their behaviors and responses.

As your children begin to see how you respond to them, they will be more willing to improve their communication with you. They have observed that you are a better listener, and that you aren't as reactionary as you have been in the past.

Try this strategy the next time you start to become defensive after one of your children's remarks. Ask, "What can I learn from this situation?" God may be talking to you through your children.

❊ PRAYER ❊

Lord, I want to grow as a person, a parent, and as a child of God. Help me keep my pride and my defensive nature out of the picture when a life lesson is unfolding. I know that my life circumstances and my children and my trials and my dreams are teaching me more and more about Your nature and character. Teach me, Lord. And help me be receptive to whoever is the teacher...even when it is my child. Amen.

Keep on learning. When you feel the anger rise, take a moment to figure out the lesson in the situation. Learn, once again, what it is to forgive and to love with God's unconditional love.

Let God's promises shine on your problems.

CORRIE TEN BOOM

Never-ending Desires

I have learned to be content in
whatever circumstances I am.

—Philippians 4:11

We don't live in a society that puts a lid on anything, let alone on our desires. As a capitalistic and consuming society we strive upward toward the next level of prosperity: bigger apartments or houses, luxury cars, the next raise, fancier vacations, and more expensive toys. The creed of success says that our happiness depends upon possessions that show those around us we have succeeded. In and of itself, there is nothing wrong with owning things. When we work hard there should be rewards at the end of the path; however, we have to be careful to make sure we aren't blinded by our drive to acquire these medals we struggle so hard for. Bob and I have learned to put a limit on our desires. As a couple we have said, "This is where we stop." We don't need any bigger or better trophies to make us happy and to give life more meaning. When a person or family puts a ceiling on their desires they, in essence, are announcing to themselves and to the ones around them that they can be happy in the present.

In today's scripture, Paul is letting us know that contentment for the now is what's important—not the desires for the future. One definition of contentment is "self-sufficiency independent of external circumstances." We need to train ourselves to verbalize and live out "More isn't always better" instead of "More is going to make me happier." A ceiling on our desires will certainly cut out much of the stress that accompanies accumulating material rewards.

✽ Prayer ✽

Father God, I'm really tired of gathering things in my life in order to be happy. Thank You for helping me realize that a ceiling on desires is very attainable, and that this contentment will give me real joy. I want to learn to appreciate the now. Amen.

✽ Heart Action ✽

Come together as a family and discuss the idea of putting a ceiling on your desires.

❧ HAVE A BALL WITH TEA! ❧

A forerunner of the tea bag, the tea ball is a perforated, ball-shaped metal container. Clasp loose tea inside and place the ball in the pot or cup before the boiling water is poured. Tea balls are not recommended for regular use, because they tend to inhibit the full flavor flow of the tea, but they're convenient—and preferable to a tea bag.

Establishing Balance
in Your Home

*Let no unwholesome word proceed from your
mouth, but only such a word as is good for
edification according to the need of the moment,
so that it will give grace to those who hear.*

—Ephesians 4:29

As a young bride and mother I began to realize that my home operated smoothly when the
emotional tone was well thought out. In the first few
years of my marriage I was a reactionary to the stresses
of the family. Then I realized a little pre-arranging
gave me a head start to prevent possible sources of
stress and conflict. I learned to be proactive.

Bob and I have planned together the tone we
want our home to reflect. Both of us like controlled
chaos with interludes of soft sounds, quiet moments,
moments for reflection and purpose. We don't like to
have mass confusion with everyone running around
like chickens with their heads cut off. We expect
respect, courtesy, and politeness to be exhibited,

with an air of calm. We want to respect each other's aloneness if he or she wants or needs space.

We incorporated today's scripture into our marriage to give us that emotional climate. Together we made sure that our conversations were uplifting and said in a tone of voice that reflected kindness. Did we slip? Of course, but our idealism soon became part of our reality.

One other feature we tried to incorporate was to keep unnecessary rushing around to a minimum. In today's age it becomes very difficult not to become a taxi for everyone's activities. We were each accountable to one another to ask if we weren't rushing around too much as a family or individual. We each had that permission to ask—and to be accountable to—each other. Even today my adult children will often ask me, "Mom, don't you need to slow down?" And you know, they're generally right on! We all need some yellow lights to remind us to have balance and slow down.

❖ PRAYER ❖

Father God, You know I want to have a well-running home with a balance in the emotional tone of my family. I truly want the members of my family to find home a

place for stillness, revitalizing, stability, and
edification. Give me ways to incorporate
these characteristics into my home. Amen.

❀ Heart Action ❀

Turn off the TV during evening meals, and play soft background music during your time of togetherness. Consider introducing a family teatime after dinner as a way to unwind at the end of the day.

You Can Touch Stars

Forgetting what lies behind and reaching forward to what lies ahead, I press on toward the goal for the prize of the upward call of God in Christ Jesus.

—PHILIPPIANS 3:13-14

Have you ever considered that you are a star people can touch? Does your life light up the room when you enter? Do your children and grandchildren reflect back to you the love you give them? Do the elderly say you make a difference in their lives? Yes, you can become a star in so many areas if you will only think of life in larger terms.

We each have 24 hours in the day and seven days in the week. What are you going to do with yours? All of the great conquests of life have started as a little idea in someone's head. It's what is done with that idea that counts.

What are the deepest dreams you have? Maybe writing a song, starting a business, authoring a book, helping children, creating a new recipe? Reach out today and plan how you are going to energize that thought into reality. Don't let it fall to the ground and perish. Nurture and water it until the sunlight makes it grow.

We are elevated by our constant aspirations. As Christians we either grow, or we begin to slide backward. No one advances by accident; all achievements are reached by a dream.

Daniel H. Burnham once said, "Make no little plans, they have no magic to stir men's blood...make big plans, aim high in hope and work."

❊ PRAYER ❊

Father God, I love to look into the vastness of space to see the twinkle of Your stars. May I be able to reach out and touch their light beams. Thank You for putting aspirations in my mind. May I develop them to Your glory. Amen.

❊ HEART ACTION ❊

Write down three dreams you have. What are you going to do with them?

Stars have long been symbols of the unattainable. They should not be so. For although our physical hands cannot reach them, we can touch them in other ways.

*Let stars stand for those things which are
ideal and radiant in life; if we seek sincerely
and strive hard enough, it is not impossible
to reach them, even though the goals seem
distant at the onset. And how often do we
touch stars when we find them close by
in the shining lives of great souls, in the
sparkling universe of humanity around us?*

Esther Baldwin York

CARROT CAKE

- 2 cups flour
- 2 teaspoons baking powder
- 1½ teaspoons baking soda
- 2 tablespoons cinnamon
- 1 teaspoon salt
- 2 cups sugar
- 1½ cups canola oil
- 4 eggs
- 2 cups grated carrots
- 1 cup crushed pineapple (drained)
- 1 cup chopped nuts (pecans or walnuts)

Preheat oven to 350° F. Mix all the above ingredients and pour into a 9 x 13 x 2 pan. Bake for 35 to 45 minutes or until toothpick comes out clean. Top with buttercream icing when cool.

BUTTERCREAM ICING

- 2 tablespoons milk
- 1 cup butter (2 cubes)
- 1 8-ounce package cream cheese
- 1 teaspoon vanilla
- 1 16-ounce box powdered sugar

Beat together all ingredients until smooth. Frost cooled cake.

❖ ❖ ❖

It is very strange, this domination of our intellect by our digestive organs. We cannot work, we cannot think, unless our stomach wills so. It dictates to us our emotions, our passions. After eggs and bacon it says, "Work!" After beefsteak and porter, it says, "Sleep!" After a cup of tea (two spoonfuls for each cup, and don't let it stand for more than three minutes), it says to the brain, "Now rise, and show your strength."

JEROME K. JEROME

This Little Light of Mine

No one, after lighting a lamp, puts it away in a cellar nor under a basket, but on the lampstand, so that those who enter may see the light.

—LUKE 11:33

Several centuries ago in a certain mountain village in Europe (so the story goes), a nobleman wondered what legacy to leave his townspeople. At last he decided to build them a church.

Nobody saw the complete plans until the church was finished. When the people gathered, they marveled at its beauty. But one noticed an incompleteness.

"Where are the lamps?" he asked. "How will the church be lighted?"

The nobleman smiled. Then he gave each family a lamp. "Each time you are here, the area in which you sit will be lighted. But when you are not here, some part of God's house will be dark."

Today we live in a world of darkness, dim paths on which even the best secular problem-solvers are beginning to stumble. In spite of our social conscience, all around us is evidence of ignorance, illiteracy, and wicked imaginings.

The world is so big, and our lamps are so small. Yes—but we can light some small part of each day. Look to the star-spangled heavens. How small each star looks in the distance. Yet, put together, those tiny jewels can light the darkest night.

Each of us is a star (or a lamp, if you will). We can make this world a brighter place. It all begins with the desire expressed in a prayer attributed to Michelangelo: "God, grant me the desire always to desire to be more than I can ever accomplish."

❧ PRAYER ❧

Father God, You are my lamp, and may I always reflect Your love to the dark world as I pass through. I trust my life is a radiant light that other people might be guided to You. I want to keep my lamp full of oil so my path will be lit by Your glow. Amen.

❧ HEART ACTION ❧

Light your lamp. Let God send you in a new direction today. Meet someone at the crossroads of his or her life and share your light. Don't be worried about their response—just be true about sharing your heart and your life.

Teapot is on, the cups are waiting,
Favorite chairs anticipating,
No matter what I have to do,
My friend, there's always time for you.

UNKNOWN

Live in Peace

*Lord, you establish peace for us; all that we
have accomplished you have done for us.*

ISAIAH 26:12 NIV

There are only a few things in life that can
truly be controlled by us. One of these is what
we do when the phone rings. You have the power
to control this intrusion into your family's life. As
we look around, we see we have become slaves to
the telephone. The other day I was dining in a fine
restaurant with a friend, when we were disturbed
by a very boisterous gentleman on a cell phone. He
made everyone around his table aware that he was
far more important than we were because he had no
consideration for our being deprived of an enjoyable
experience at lunch.

How many times has the phone rung while your
family was having a quiet meal together? Everyone
looks anxiously at each other, wondering who will
bolt to the phone to see who's calling. Don't answer
the phone at mealtime unless you are expecting an
emergency phone call. Let the family know that they

are much more important than the unknown person at the other end of the line. Yes, there are certain situations when you don't need to answer the phone.

I've been known to switch off the ringer on the phone during important times of the evening. This way we don't hear the rings and aren't inclined to interrupt our evening time together. The answering machine or voice mail will pick up the message, and we can reply at a more convenient time.

Certainly there will be times when we need to answer the phone, but *you* decide when. Don't let others control your life and alter your scheduled activities. Ask yourself, "Is my life going to be made easier or will there be more stress by answering the phone whenever it rings?" You have the power to decide.

❋ PRAYER ❋

Father God, prevent me from automatically being a slave to the phone. Empower me to make that decision. There are times and occasions when I want to say no. Who says that all calls must be answered personally right away! Amen.

❋ Heart Action ❋

For one week don't answer the telephone during dinnertime. You'll discover a more peaceful family time together.

The morning cup of coffee has an exhilaration about it which the cheering influence of the afternoon or evening cup of tea cannot be expected to reproduce.

Oliver Wendell Holmes Sr.

The Haven of Home

By wisdom a house is built, and by
understanding it is established; and by
knowledge the rooms are filled with
all precious and pleasant riches.

—PROVERBS 24:3-4

A home is a man's castle. It is a place where weary and tired journeyers find peace and quiet after a long day of travels. We don't protect this structure because we are selfish, but because we don't want the craziness of the world to enter within the walls and destroy the restorations that a calm and peaceful home provides for those who live inside. It is one of the only places left where a man and his family can turn away the cares of the world. My husband, Bob, used to tell me he couldn't wait to get home in the evening, because it held so much comfort within its walls.

The home is where your privacy can be protected. You can set the atmosphere and interactions any way you want, including…

- keeping a quiet spirit that's reflected in the home

- talking politely at all times
- using courteous manners
- having soothing music playing
- choosing not to answer the phone while enjoying meals or special times together

You and your family need to decide how your quiet times will be protected. We have a saying around our home, "Say *no* to good things, and save your *yeses* for the best." When you enter your home, know that it is yours, not someone else's. No matter how small or how large your house might be, let your privacy reign supreme.

❊ Prayer ❊

Lord, let me continue to preserve the privacy of my home. May I take the time to protect what comes into the house so only those things that give peace and tranquility to my family can come in. Make my home a place where the occupants can find freedom from the struggles of the world. Amen.

❊ Heart Action ❊

Get together as a family and discuss ways to make your home a safe haven amid the world's chaos.

Home is the one place in all this world where hearts are sure of each other. It is the place of confidence. It is the place where we tear off that mask of guarded and suspicious coldness which the world forces us to wear in self-defense, and where we pour out the unreserved communication of full and confiding hearts. It is the spot where expressions of tenderness gush out without any dread of sensation of awkwardness and without any dread of ridicule.

Frederick W. Robertson

The Ritual of Tea

*Hospitality should have
no other nature than love.*

HENRIETTA MEARS

Have you ever noticed that your mind seems to work better when your body is occupied with something it's done before—like taking a walk or washing dishes or mowing the lawn? The same thing happens to me when I'm rinsing out a teapot or cutting the crust off little sandwiches or arranging tea things on a tray. The little repetitive actions of preparing and serving tea become the reassuring soil out of which thoughts can grow and conversations can spring.

There's no hurry about any of this, since you can't go ahead with the tea until the water is boiling. And there's more waiting to do even then, because the tea leaves or tea bags must steep in the pot. But while you are waiting for the liquid to turn its fragrant amber, you can carry the tray to a comfortable nook and wait in peace. If you are with friends, this is a wonderful time to reconnect with one another. If you are alone, you can read or think or pray or just "be."

The brewed tea is too hot to sip quickly, but it will cool. You can simply sit and wait until the boiling liquid settles into comfortable warmth. Maybe you can read yet another page of your book. Or you can politely pass the cream and sugar and cookies or fruit to your friends—more ritual.

Then your cup is ready to enjoy. And somehow, as you sip, your mind continues to settle down from its habitual rush. Your words and your musings slow down and sink deeper. Your relationships—even your relationship with yourself—are granted space for a leisurely stretch. And the beautiful thing is, all this slowdown takes so little time!

Enjoying a cup of tea is not like taking a summer off or going away on a retreat. It's an island of calm you can reasonably visit in the course of your busiest day.

In this sense, I think taking tea is a bit like riding a train. The trip from Southern California, where we live, to Chicago by passenger rail requires several solid days, and unforeseen delays may stretch the journey even longer. If you worry constantly about "when we're going to get there," you'll be a nervous wreck, but you won't get there any faster.

Yet if you adjust your jet-age expectations to the rhythm of the rails, taking train travel on its own terms, you begin to discover unexpected pleasures. You can walk freely through the aisles or relax in big, comfortable seats. You can enjoy a meal in the dining car or talk to people in the club car or just sit and watch the scenery.

Once you make the decision to adjust your pace, you can relax and enjoy the journey.

Tea is like that too. You may need to change your mental gears to enjoy it fully. You may need to practice waiting and learning to enjoy the repetitive freedom of the ritual. But once you do, the change of pace will renew your mind and refresh your spirit.

❁ PRAYER ❁

Lord, give me a heart for the ritual
of giving and serving. May I follow
Your example every day. Amen.

❁ HEART ACTION ❁

Make room in your life to serve others.

Lemon Bites

Shells:
- 1 cup all-purpose flour
- ½ cup finely chopped pecans
- ¼ cup sugar
- 1 egg
- ¼ cup softened butter (½ stick)

Filling:
- 1 teaspoon unflavored gelatin
- 1 tablespoon cold water
- 2 eggs
- ½ cup sugar
- 2 tablespoons grated lemon zest
- ¼ cup fresh lemon juice
- 2 tablespoons butter
- whipped cream and additional grated lemon zest for garnish

For the shells, preheat the oven to 375° F. Mix the flour, pecans, and sugar in a bowl. Add the egg and butter, and mix until crumbly.

Press the dough onto the bottoms and sides of ungreased miniature muffin cups. Bake 10 minutes or until light golden brown. Remove pans to a wire rack to cool.

For the filling, soften the gelatin in the cold water in a saucepan. Beat the eggs and sugar in a bowl. Stir into the gelatin mixture and bring to a boil, stirring constantly. Reduce heat, simmer for 10 minutes. Remove from the heat and stir in the lemon zest, lemon juice, and butter. Pour the filling into baked shells. Chill for 1 hour or until set. Remove from the muffin cups to a serving platter. Garnish with whipped cream and lemon zest. Makes 24.

A friend told me recently to save the first Saturday in January. She's planning a tea to celebrate her spiritual birthday, and she wants her special friends to join her. Having tea together nurtures friendship by inviting us to be present—right now, in the moment. So much in our culture can be done without really being there—without being mentally and emotionally tuned in to the people around us. There's something about an old-fashioned tea party that gently invites us to feel safe—it's comforting, inviting. Believe me, it's not the tea! It's the *spirit* of the tea party. Take the time to enjoy the time with kindred spirits over a cup of tea! It's both simple and wonderful.

"Mom, I'm Bored!"

*All discipline for the moment seems not
to be joyful, but sorrowful; yet to those
who have been trained by it, afterwards it
yields the peaceful fruit of righteousness.*

—Hebrews 12:11

One of the phrases that used to really bug me when the children were at home was "Mom, I'm bored!" Then I had the responsibility to think of some creative way to entertain them. Wrong! Today's children have had so much overstimulation by the multitude of choices available that when there is a quiet moment they find themselves without something to do—so they think they are bored. Over the years I realized there is nothing wrong with "being bored." We don't have to fall into the trap of thinking we must fill every moment with activities. In reality, we don't have to "do"; we have to learn to "be."

Let the children solve their own problems of inactivity. They have to learn to be problem-solvers because you won't always be around to give them suggestions on what to do. However, you can be a model of what to do with those few precious down-times during the day: read a book, listen to good music, write a letter, make a batch of cookies, or crawl up on the sofa and take a 20-minute nap.

Don't try to entertain or stimulate your children out of their boredom. It's their responsibility to be creative. But you can help them understand that an activity won't always solve the boredom problem. There's nothing wrong if we aren't doing something every moment of the day. Time to relax is okay.

We all need to learn how to live with quiet times. Teach your kids to take them as gifts from heaven. Show them how they can use them to recharge their batteries.

Make your personal prayer and devotional time something your kids understand is a priority. They will witness how quiet time becomes something that enriches a person's life.

❋ PRAYER ❋

Father God, thanks for giving me those
quiet times during the day—let me teach
my children to use these minutes as a time to
rest and enjoy life. Let me show them how to
create and get the most out of these quiet times.

*May my family look at boredom as a great
opportunity to rest in Your presence. Amen.*

❁ HEART ACTION ❁

Think of how you can share the joy of downtime
the next time your children come to you and say,
"Mom, we're bored."

*At times our own light goes out and is rekindled
by a spark from another person. Each of us
has cause to think with deep gratitude of
those who have lighted the flame within us.*

ALBERT SCHWEITZER

Virtue of Timeliness

Wisdom is a tree of life to those who embrace
her; happy are those who hold her tightly.

—Proverbs 3:18 nlt

My Bob has the great virtue of always being on
time. Our son, Brad, once asked him, "Dad,
aren't you ever late?" His question was a compliment
for timeliness. Being on time is certainly a virtue. We
can prioritize our appointments so we aren't stressed
trying to get to them. I have found that if I allow
myself at least ten extra minutes between activities, I
have a greater sense of peace. That last-minute push
to catch up for that next activity is what can drive us
crazy—and it can mean the difference between a good
day or a bad day. I tell myself that I'm going to be 10
minutes early. That way, I have a few extra minutes to
arrive refreshed instead of stressed and haggard.

Think about how you or some of your family
members procrastinate when it comes time to actually get out the front door. Do you leave getting ready
until the last minute because you are trying to get
three other people dressed and organized? Delegate to

them their own responsibilities so everyone, including you, has a chance to be on time. Model organization and calmness so your family follows this example when it is time to go to school or church or an evening activity. If you have kids who are different ages, have the older ones help the younger ones.

Patience and timeliness come along when wisdom is put into play. It might take some practice. When you and your family are on time, you all will enjoy the day rather than rushing through life helter-skelter.

❊ Prayer ❊

Father God, You know I don't want chaos in my life. I beg of You to help me be 10 minutes early for my appointments. I don't like my gut feeling when I'm running late to the next activity. I don't want to be behind. I really want to be early. Amen.

❊ Heart Action ❊

Don't overschedule your activities. Leave a little time between each activity. Allow for some downtime by scheduling breaks.

*Finish every day and be done with it. You
have done what you could. Some blunders
and absurdities no doubt crept in; forget
them as soon as you can. Tomorrow is a new
day; begin it well and serenely, and with
too high a spirit to be cumbered with your
old nonsense. This day is all that is good
and fair. It is too dear with its hopes and
invitations, to waste a moment on yesterday.*

EMERSON

APPLE CIDER TEA

- 2½ teaspoons black tea leaves
- 2½ cups water
- ¼ cup sugar
- juice of 2 oranges (about 1 cup)
- 5 cups apple cider
- 8 thin lemon slices

Following the traditional method, make tea from tea leaves and boiling water; allow to brew for 5 minutes. Place sugar in a large bowl or pitcher. Strain hot tea into bowl and stir until sugar is dissolved. Stir in orange juice. Just before serving, add apple cider and reheat. Pour into cups and offer slices of lemon. Serve hot or cold.

FAVORITE TEA SANDWICHES

Cucumber sandwiches are perhaps most commonly associated with afternoon tea. Peel cucumbers and slice very thin. Sprinkle slices with salt and drain on paper towels. Spread white bread with unsalted butter and a thin layer of cream cheese and layer cucumbers no more than ¼ inch thick. Cut into desired shapes.

Watercress sandwiches are also favorite tea-party fare. Butter white or rye bread and fill with watercress leaves. Cut into squares, arrange on plate, and garnish with watercress.

❋ ❋ ❋

We had a kettle; we let it leak:
Our not repairing made it worse.
We haven't had any tea for a week…
The bottom is out of the Universe.

RUDYARD KIPLING

A Spot That Wouldn't Go Away

*If we confess our sins, He is faithful and
righteous to forgive us our sins and to
cleanse us from all unrighteousness.*

—1 John 1:9

One day, after a busy morning of painting our wrought-iron fence green, Bob came into the house to eat lunch. He thought he had cleaned up adequately, but he had missed one spot on his right elbow. As he rested his elbow on my recently cleaned white quilted tablecloth, he noticed that a spot of green paint had been transferred onto it. Immediately, he knew he was in trouble. He soaked a rag with paint thinner and used some elbow grease, but to no avail. The spot would not disappear. He tried again and again, but it was still visible.

To this date, the green stain still appears to remind me that sin is that way in our lives. Once it has tainted my soul, I can try and try to remove it, but it stays until I go to the cross and ask for forgiveness from God. I know that Jesus died on the cross for all my sins—past, present, and future. What a wonderful assurance to know that I have the best stain remover in the universe with Jesus!

If we still carry the heavy burden of sin around, it affects our radiance, confidence, emotional stability, and physical well-being. Much of our dysfunction is because we haven't learned to ask Jesus to carry our sins for us.

If you are one of those people who carry around a heavy load of transgressions, you can be forgiven today. Take on a new life by asking Jesus to come into your life! He will lift from your shoulders the weight of sin that won't go away.

❃ Prayer ❃

Lord, I ask You to step in and forgive me of all my sins. I'm tired of trying to clean up my life all by myself. I have no more strength left. Help me give my sins and my life to You every day. Amen.

❃ Heart of Action ❃

Seek to forgive others today so you can understand the beauty of the power of forgiveness. Immerse yourself in an understanding of God's grace and let it fill you and overflow to other people.

All true tea lovers
not only like their tea strong,
but like it a little stronger
with each year that passes.

GEORGE ORWELL

A perfect temperature for tea is two
degrees hotter than perfect.

TERRI GUILLEMETZ

Let Your Home Reflect Love

A house is built of logs and stone,
of tiles and posts and piers;
A home is built of loving deeds
that stand a thousand years.

—Victor Hugo

I can't walk in my front door without seeing evidences of love. Everywhere I look I'm reminded that Bob and I have created a home in which you're going to get loved. As you walk up the path to the front door, you see roses, a rose arbor, potted plants with welcome signs everywhere. As you enter, you see uplifting signs of encouragement, pictures hanging that reflect our family values, and a coffee table filled with family pictures dating back five generations. Even though many have passed on, their names are familiar to the grandchildren because we talk of them as if they're still alive.

The furniture says, "Welcome—you can come and sit on me. It's okay if you mess up the pillows."

There is an abundance of freshly cut flowers that release sweet-smelling fragrances of nature. In the kitchen all kinds of children's art hang on the front of the refrigerator. The grandchildren love to furnish the latest of their designs for display in our home.

The refrigerator is open for tiny hands to check out its contents. They can always find the ingredients for their favorite treats. The adults who filter in find fresh drink and soothing music that relaxes stress and tension.

People often comment how relaxed and loved they feel in our home. It's almost impossible not to feel loved when you are in a setting that says, "I love you."

Does your home reflect God's love and provision? Is it an oasis of peace? Pay attention to what your home and your heart say to others. Live well and fully and with great kindness that invites others to a sanctuary of comfort.

❋ PRAYER ❋

Father God, thank You for showing me how I can show Your love in my home. We don't always have to say, "I love you" aloud, even though that's important. The nonverbal language is just as effective. Amen.

❖ Heart Action ❖

Do something to your home that says "I love you!"

The measure of a happy life is not from the fewer or more suns to behold, the fewer or more breaths we draw, or meals we repeat, but from having once lived well, acted our part handsomely, and made our exit cheerfully.

Lord Shaftesbury

Stay Loose and Strong

She sets about her work vigorously;
her arms are strong for her tasks.

PROVERBS 31:17 NIV

As you know, I'm known for organization, to-do lists, organization charts, appointments, and doing more than one thing at a time, but there are times when you have children at home that you need to stay loose. As most of you have probably already experienced, rigidity can be a negative when raising children. When you have all your i's dotted and your t's crossed, you end up with a lot of disappointments due to false expectations. You start out the day with a full agenda, and soon it's noon and nothing has been checked off your list. Sometimes with children that's the way it goes. Hang loose and keep on plugging away. What doesn't get done today can slide over until tomorrow. There are times when we must accomplish certain tasks, but in general rigidity causes a lot of stress in our lives.

Being rigid keeps you from making good choices.

Being strong helps you handle what life brings your way.

Don't let your mind tell you that you are ineffective. Relax and be assured that you're okay as a wife and mom. Try to be looser and less rigid, and laugh more. Show your strength and love by embracing life instead of trying to control every aspect of it.

What you do and what you share today is not always going to have a direct result or an immediate benefit. That's why you have to stay loose as you let a day unfold and see what kinds of great things emerge. Let yourself enjoy the future pleasure of seeing how these efforts pay off down the road in the hearts and lives of your children.

❈ PRAYER ❈

Father God, let me be looser with my daily agendas. Help me try to give myself a lot of latitude as I raise my children. Keep the guilt trip out of my mind. With children, I want to concentrate on the now, and not on a stuffed-full program each day. Amen.

❈ HEART ACTION ❈

Work on this mind-set. Stay flexible with today's agenda; go with the flow.

I shot an arrow into the air,
It fell to earth, I knew not where;
For, so swiftly it flew, the sight
Could not follow it in its flight.

I breathed a song into the air,
It fell to earth, I knew not where;
For who has sight so keen and strong,
That it can follow the flight of song?

Long, long afterward, in an oak
I found the arrow, still unbroke;
And the song, from beginning to end,
I found again in the heart of a friend.

—Henry Wadsworth Longfellow

Conformed Versus Transformed

Do not be conformed to this world, but be transformed by the renewing of your mind, so that you may prove what the will of God is, that which is good and acceptable and perfect.

—ROMANS 12:2

Have you ever asked, "What is the will of God for my life?" I know I have many times. This question seems like the biggest mystery of the Christian walk.

How do I move forward? I have used this passage from Romans 12 as a help to first make me realize that there is a tremendous battle going on in my mind between good and evil, right and wrong, godly and ungodly. This verse is a reminder regarding that battle. I always want to be in God's will and not my own. I must open my mind to realize that the world (secular thinking) is trying to win me over to its side. However, the warning in Romans is to not be conformed, but be *transformed* by the renewing of my mind so I can…

- know what the will of God is
- learn what is good, acceptable, and perfect

A companion verse to help me in this transformation of the mind is found in Philippians 4:8, which reads,

> Whatever is true, whatever is honorable, whatever is right, whatever is pure, whatever is lovely, whatever is of good repute, if there is any excellence and if anything worthy of praise, dwell on these things.

I can assure you that if you use these two verses, and if you search the Scriptures, your mind will be transformed and you'll know what the will of God is for your life. Don't forget to talk to well-respected Christians also. Their insights can be very helpful. Formulate your direction and move out. Because you are earnestly seeking God's will, if you are going in the wrong direction, He will correct your course.

❊ PRAYER ❊

Father God, I appreciate all the various
verses of Scripture You put into my heart
so I can be drawing closer to You all

the time. I'm glad You have put in my
heart a desire for goodness. Amen.

❋ HEART ACTION ❋

Write down three things you can do to transform
your life in a godly direction. Work on incorporating
these into your life.

I smile, of course,
And go on drinking tea,
Yet with these April sunsets, that somehow recall
My buried life, and Paris in the Spring,
I feel immeasurably at peace, and find the world
To be wonderful and youthful, after all.

T.S. ELIOT

Keep Your Joy Alive

*You too have grief now; but I will see you
again, and your heart will rejoice, and no
one will take your joy away from you.*

—John 16:22

Joy will always follow sorrow. I've met so many women who are right in the middle of sorrow— a death, a separation, a divorce, a serious health problem, teenage children that are rebelling, financial difficulties, an unbelieving mate. The list goes on and on.

Each of us at one time or the other has been in deep sorrow. Sometimes it seems like a smile will never appear on our faces, because the burden is so heavy and the load is so great.

When I was struggling with my illness and my heart was aching for the troubles in my daughter's life, the tears of sorrow streamed down my face and soaked my pillow. As I prayed for the situation, I pled to God to "restore to me the joy of Your salvation" (Psalm 51:12). A friend would call, I would receive a note through the mail, or a fax with a verse of

Scripture or poem would appear. And my heart and spirit would be lifted.

The load becomes lighter and I can pray to God to continue my joy even during a time of trouble. In my Bible I have a card that reads, "Don't doubt in the morning what God has promised you in the night." When you rise up in the morning with your thoughts and eyes fixed on God's promises, your attitude will not be one of fear, but one of hope.

Watch for the many confirmations and testimonies of God's love. These too will give you a renewed sense of care and contentment. And most important, don't let anyone or anything take away your joy. It is yours to have and to hold.

❊ PRAYER ❊

Father God, help me see Your beauty all around me. May my joy spill over from a cupful of "thank-Yous." Joy is a decision on my part, and I'm committed that no one can take that away from me. Amen.

❊ HEART ACTION ❊

Call a friend today who might need a reminder that God loves him or her—and that you do as well.

*Family life is full of major and minor crises—
the ups and downs of health, success, and
failure in career, marriage, and divorce—and
all kinds of characters. It is tied to places
and events and histories. With all of these
felt details, life etches itself into memory
and personality. It's difficult to imagine
anything more nourishing to the soul.*

THOMAS MOORE

Spiced Tea

- 2 medium lemons
- 1½ whole cloves
- 7 cup-sized tea bags
- 2 teaspoons whole cloves
- 2 teaspoons whole allspice
- 11 cups boiling water
- 2 cups sugar
- 1⅓ cup orange juice
- ⅔ cup lemon juice

Cut each lemon into 6 slices; stud slices with cloves. Combine tea bags and remaining spices with the boiling water in a large Dutch oven (any big kettle will do). Cover and let it steep over medium heat for 15 minutes. Remove tea bags and spices. Add sugar and orange and lemon juice. Pour tea mixture into heatproof serving bowl. Add lemon slices. Serve hot. Makes 3 quarts.

Easy Nut Bread

- 3 cups sifted flour
- 4 teaspoons baking powder
- 1 teaspoon salt
- ¾ cup sugar

Add:
- 1 unbeaten egg
- 1½ cups milk
- ¼ cup melted shortening
- 1 cup chopped nuts (your choice)

Sift flour once before measuring. Melt and cool shortening. Grease 4 x 8 loaf pan. Mix together the first 4 ingredients. Beat the next 4 items until they are mixed together. Make a hole in the dry ingredients and pour the liquids together. Mix until well blended. Pour into greased pan. Let stand 20 minutes. Preheat oven to 350° F. Bake for 1 hour and 10 minutes or until golden brown and firm to the touch. Flavor improves if baked at least a day ahead of time. Makes 1 large loaf.

Friendship Appreciation

I count myself in nothing else so happy
As in a soul rememb'ring my good friends.

WILLIAM SHAKESPEARE

It is one of the most important lessons we learn in life: We should always take care of the things we love. That's especially true of our treasured friendships. If we want them to last and grow, we need to invest some time and energy and thought into nurturing and maintaining them.

It was the Duchess of Bedford who first thought of tea and cakes to carry her through until dinnertime. A lot of time has passed since then—but some things do grow better with age. For me, tea is connected to many special times I've had alone with God, in the presence of family, and among dear old friends and precious new ones.

But what is it—besides the occasional tea party—that keeps friendships alive and well? A lot of it just comes naturally. As we spend time together and enjoy each other's company and help each other, we're also taking care of our relationships. And yet a little deliberate nurturing goes a long way toward keeping a friendship in full bloom.

Most of the time, a little everyday tending is all that is needed—a phone call or an e-mail, a touch or a hug, a thoughtful present, a silly surprise, or just a quiet cup of tea together. Such little gifts and gestures between friends keep us connected. So do the sacrifices we are willing to make for each other. And so does the willingness to address problems that arise between you, to talk the matter out or let it go and forgive.

Most of all, nurturing a friendship involves keeping each other in mind—even when we're not together. It means checking in on a regular basis, just to share our hearts and make sure that everything is all right. It means seeking out ways to communicate in ways little and large.

Remember—true friends accept each other, honor each other, and care for each other.

❊ PRAYER ❊

Lord, I thank You for the gift of friendship.
May I always nurture and value the
relationships You bring into my life. Amen.

❖ HEART ACTION ❖

Take care of a friend you love today. Call her. Express your appreciation of her and make time to listen to what is going on in her life.

Women are like tea bags.
We don't know our true strength
until we're in hot water.

NANCY REAGAN

How Do I Pray?

*O Lord, hear me praying; listen to
my plea, O God my King, for I will
never pray to anyone but you.*

—Psalm 5:1 TLB

Have you ever thought, *What's the proper posture while I pray? Is it all right if I pray while I'm standing at the sink washing dishes? What about when I'm doing my other chores? If I pray then, will God hear me as well as when I'm on my knees in a quiet room?* In searching for the answers in the Word of God, we've discovered that all positions are appropriate for prayer. God gives great liberty to praying people. The important issue is that our hearts are in communion with Him as we pray. In Scripture, we discover many ways of praying:

- kneeling (1 Kings 8:54; Ezra 9:5; Daniel 6:10; Acts 20:36)
- standing (Jeremiah 18:20)
- sitting (2 Samuel 7:18)
- in bed (Psalm 63:6)

- in private (Matthew 6:6; Mark 1:35)
- with others (Psalm 35:18)
- hands lifted (1 Timothy 2:8)
- silently (1 Samuel 1:13)
- loudly (Acts 16:25)
- at all times (Luke 18:1)

How do you prepare your heart to enter God's presence? Are you able to pause during your day long enough to calm your heart, settle your worries, let go of the to-do list, and be still?

If you struggle to quiet your heart and want to spend some focused time in prayer, let tea become your way to do just that. Give it a try. Place the kettle, prepare your cup, and settle into a time of quiet. Take a sip or two of tea and then close your eyes. You will be more ready to talk to God and to listen to Him.

You can pray anytime and anywhere. You can have chaos going on all around you. You can be feeling strong and healthy or frail and sick. Life might be going along smoothly, or it might be one of the rockiest patches you've ever experienced. Prayer doesn't depend on circumstances. It depends on you showing up to talk to God...no matter where you are. You can count on Him being right there, by your side, in your heart, and ready to listen.

❊ PRAYER ❊

Father God, as I fulfill my calling as a believer who loves You, please hear my every prayer—no matter what position I assume. Amen.

❊ HEART ACTION ❊

During the next week, try several different positions as you pray. Read the Scripture given above that goes with each position.

The Comfort of Tea

You make a living by what you get.
You make a life by what you give.

WINSTON CHURCHILL

Collecting teacups in Southern California is really an act of faith. I recall the time we had a major earthquake not far from where I live. Our home was safely south of the epicenter, and my tea things were safe, but friends and acquaintances showed me heart-stopping photographs of knee-deep rubble. Days of shaking and aftershocks left all their breakable treasures in shards and shatters.

It wouldn't take much of an earthquake to send all my teacups crashing to the floor.

Actually, it wouldn't take an earthquake at all, for my fragile teacups are also vulnerable to more mundane dangers—the cat, the feather duster, my grandchildren, my own carelessness.

I always have to confess that once I broke 14 of my own prized teacups! A glass shelf was balanced precariously after cleaning, and it collapsed at my accidental nudge. More than a dozen of my favorite cups fell and broke to smithereens.

I was so devastated I couldn't face what had happened. I simply swept the china shards into a box and put in on the shelf—and six years passed before I could muster the courage to look inside the box. Only one cup was in large enough pieces even to be salvaged with glue, and it will never be the same.

All this is to say that I take a significant risk in keeping my teacups out. I take a risk in using them, in letting others use them. But it's a risk I choose to take. I choose it with my eyes open, and I choose it with gladness.

After all, life is fragile too.

But if we let that risk stop us from living, we've already lost! While protecting ourselves from injury and loss, we're also cutting ourselves off from joy and growth. But life in all its vulnerable beauty is incomparably worth it.

It is this realization that has taught me to take risks with my teacups, to avoid the temptation to fall back on "safe" mugs or even paper cups. I've even learned to take those teacups traveling—outdoors on our grounds, on a picnic, or even in a basket to visit a friend. Once I move past the "safety" mentality, I can use my beautiful tea things as they were intended—to share joy and friendship and caring, truly a "cup of kindness." I can be thankful that something meaningful to me can give comfort to another.

Humans are beautiful and breakable, like china cups…yet we are also strong and resilient. And unlike my cups, humans can heal and grow and move beyond disaster. We can reach out to one another in courage and comfort.

So what will I do when another earthquake comes?

I guess I'll do what anyone must do when disaster strikes: I'll pick up the pieces.

And then, somehow, I'll have another cup of tea.

❊ PRAYER ❊

God, help me be a compassionate, giving
person who is quick to offer up comfort and
beauty. Let me not worry about "things"
so that I can focus on hearts. Amen.

❊ HEART ACTION ❊

Take your best tea items out of their protective wrapping or out of the cabinet and use them today.

❋ THE PORTABLE TEA PARTY ❋

Here's what to pack for a traveling tea party:

- large basket with handle
- tea cloth and serviettes (you can make these yourself from print fabric or sheets)
- 2 teacups and saucers
- 2 tea plates
- 2 dessert forks
- small dish for butter or other spread
- 2 or 3 small serving plates
- 1 four-cup teapot (if basket is going to a place where hot water is available)
- Thermos bottle (if you are taking your tea on a picnic)
- tea strainer
- butter knife
- 2 teaspoons
- tea foods (don't forget butter and spreads)
- cream, lemon wedges, and lumps of sugar
- tea
- candleholder and candle

- matches
- small vase and silk flowers
- several tea towels (use to wrap breakable items)

Pack the tea cloth last, use it to cover the top of the basket.

❊ An Afternoon Custom ❊

Traditional English tea is an afternoon affair, served anytime between three and six o'clock—and the later in the day it occurs, the more hearty the offerings. But there's no law that says you can't enjoy a warming cup with friends—and a delightful time of fellowship—any time of the day, even for breakfast or a nightcap.

TICKLE ME PINK
RASPBERRY ICED TEA

This cold tea drink is refreshing any time of the year.

- 6 cups boiling water
- ½ cup lightly packed fresh mint leaves or 7 bags of herbal mint tea
- 4 cups cold water
- 2 12-ounce containers frozen lemonade concentrate
- 1 cup frozen raspberries

In a teapot, pour boiling water over tea bags; cover and steep 5 minutes. Remove the bags. Place frozen lemonade concentrate in a heatproof pitcher and pour some of the hot mint tea over it; stir until lemonade is thawed. Add 4 cups cold water, ice, and raspberries before serving.

Take Great and Little Things to Him

*Let the children alone, and do not
hinder them from coming to Me.*

—Matthew 19:14

Childlike confidence makes us pray as nothing else can. It causes a person to pray for great things they would never have asked for if they hadn't learned this simple assurance. We think that our great things are somehow worthy of God's attention—in reality, our biggest petitions are little to God. In turn, we think our little things must be so small that it is not worth His time to bother with them.

Instead, we need to realize that what is important to a child may be very small to his parent, and yet the parent measures the request, not from his own point of view but from the child's. Have you ever heard your little child cry bitterly and you hurried over to find out what was wrong? Upon examination, you discovered the cause of the pain was a small splinter in his finger. While you did not need to call a surgeon to take the splinter out, the injury was a great thing to your small youngster. Standing there with his eyes all wet with tears of pain, your son never imagined that his pain was too insignificant for you to care about. What are mothers and fathers made for but to look after the small concerns of their little children?

God, our Father, is a good father who pities us as human fathers pity their children. He counts the stars and calls them by name, yet He also hears and heals the brokenhearted and binds up our wounds. If you have put your confidence in God, you will take great concerns and little concerns to Him, knowing He will always respond. He has said that those who trust Him "will not be disappointed" (1 Peter 2:6).

God always hears the prayers of a loving person because those prayers reflect who He is.

❊ Prayer ❊

Father God, little or big, I bring my needs before You. If You number the sands on the beach, You are surely interested in the details of my life. Thank You for majoring on the minors of life. You are an awesome God. Amen.

❋ Heart Action ❋

Cry out to God. Praise Him for the smallest and greatest of blessings. And cry for help in the midst of the smallest and greatest struggles. Never hesitate to reveal a small need in your life. God's promises will cover you in all things.

Remember the tea kettle—it is always up to its neck in hot water, yet it still sings!

Unknown

The Most Important Question

*Pilate said to them, "Then what shall I
do with Jesus who is called Christ?"*

—MATTHEW 27:22

When I was a young girl, I loved watching the
television show *The $64,000 Question*. The
contestants would be asked various questions. If one
of them was successful in answering correctly over
a period of weeks, that person could potentially win
$64,000. I loved watching them try each week. Then,
to my disappointment, a scandal broke that charged
the producer of the show with leaking answers to
the contestants so they could win. I had so wanted
to believe in the people who were answering the big
questions.

Years later, when I was dating Bob, I would be
confronted with the most basic, fundamental, and
important question in *my* life. After coming home
one evening from a wonderful date, he asked me the
same question that Pilate asked the crowd in today's
Scripture reading: "What shall I do with Jesus who is

called Christ?" I had never been asked that question. I had recently graduated from Hebrew school; Jesus wasn't exactly a name to be discussed in my circle.

I asked, "What do you mean? Why do I need to answer that question? I'm not a sinner. I'm a good Jewish girl, and I have no need for Him. I believe in God."

I knew Bob was a Christian and believed differently than I did, but what did Jesus have to do with it? Bob could see how perplexed I was, and so he gently began to share with me who this Jesus was and the full gospel of the birth, life, and resurrection of Jesus. He lovingly shared the plan of salvation with me and told me he would pray for me regarding the answer to the big question I now faced. In the weeks that followed, Bob asked my mother if he could take me to church. My sweet mother surprised us all and said yes.

At church, I heard teaching from Scripture that made me ask questions I had never thought about before. Then one night, I was lying in bed, and that question popped into my mind: "What shall I do with Jesus who is called Christ?" And I knew how to answer it. I asked Jesus to come into my life, to forgive me of my sins, to become my Lord and my Messiah.

The rewards of that response were worth far more

than $64,000! How do you answer that question: "What shall I do with Jesus who is called Christ?"

❧ PRAYER ❧

God, I'm so thankful that I have been asked the big question and that my heart shouted "yes" to You. Amen.

❧ HEART ACTION ❧

Ask yourself the most important question of all: "What shall *I* do with Jesus who is called Christ?"

No Busy Signals

I want the men in every place to pray, lifting
up holy hands, without wrath and dissension.

—1 Timothy 2:8

Prayer is honored by our Lord, and we are commanded and told to have personal communion with Him. It is not something we have to do, but something we *get* to do. *What a privilege!* We need not make an appointment to get His attention. He is truly a 24/7 God; He is *always* available. Psalm 145:18 supports that truth: "The Lord is near to all who call upon Him." We aren't screened by an answering machine, caller ID, an administrative assistant, or a group of secretaries. Nope. God is always there for us. He never is too busy. He will never say, "Call back when My calendar isn't so full." We are invited to walk boldly into His presence at any moment, day or night. Scripture tells us that we are known by Him. Just think, God knows our names. Truly, His invitation to prayer is a precious expression of His love for each one of us. Here are a few verses of Scripture that might help us know more about this wonderful opportunity to pray.

- "Seek the LORD and His strength; seek His face continually" (1 Chronicles 16:11).
- "The prayer of the upright is His delight" (Proverbs 15:8).
- Jesus told His disciples a parable "to show that at all times they ought to pray and not to lose heart" (Luke 18:1).
- "The Spirit also helps our weakness; for we do not know how to pray as we should, but the Spirit Himself intercedes for us with groanings too deep for words" (Romans 8:26).
- "Be anxious for nothing, but in everything by prayer and supplication with thanksgiving let your requests be made known to God" (Philippians 4:6).

Nurture a prayer life that leads you into God's presence frequently. It will become your first response when you face the joys and the struggles in your life. Keep God on your mind and in your heart throughout the day. You will discover how easy it becomes to seek Him and His guidance in every matter, big or small.

❖ PRAYER ❖

Father God, thank You for inviting me

*into Your presence. You are a God who is
concerned about me. I love Your kindness and
Your desire to hear my every need. Amen.*

❖ HEART ACTION ❖

Choose one of the listed scriptures to meditate on today. Thank the Lord for giving us a way to communicate with Him. Praise God for prayer.

*One sip of this will bathe the drooping spirits
in delight, beyond the bliss of dreams.*

MILTON

Be Content to Wait a Little

You have covered Yourself with a cloud
so that no prayer can pass through.

—LAMENTATIONS 3:44

Wait upon the Lord! We pray for patience, and God answers our prayers. We have learned to wait in lines at the bank, at the checkout counter, at the Department of Motor Vehicles, and at ball games. Wait, wait, wait. All we get to do is wait. So when it comes to answered prayers, we don't want to wait. We want it in our time, not God's time. We don't have a hundred years. Lord, *now* is the appointed time.

Two of our all-time favorite friends, George and Ruth, were much older than us at the time of our friendship. We looked up to them as models of dignity. They were both tall and very attractive. Ruth was our example of a truly feminine lady—elegant in all areas of life. George was a Cary Grant look-alike. He was a very successful oil tycoon, and often his vocabulary slipped and out came "roughneck language," to the embarrassment of Ruth. She would blush and say, "Oh, George." Not until we got to know them better did we learn that Ruth had earnestly prayed for George's salvation for 35 years. Here was a lady who was willing to wait for God's timing. Later in life, George did come to know Jesus as his Lord. What a day of celebration that was for all who loved him.

We always recall Ruth's faithful endurance when we lose patience with God and want an answer on our schedule. God's timing is always better than ours. Is there something you've been waiting for a response for? Do you pray, like Ruth, for another's salvation? An unexpressed desire of your heart? A life-direction uncertainty that needs resolution?

Don't be discouraged when you face your unanswered prayers. We are dealing with a God to whom a day is like a thousand years and a thousand years is like a day. His timepiece is greater than a Rolex watch. Unanswered prayer doesn't mean He hasn't heard. In His proper timing, He will give you an answer. Keep those longtime prayers lifted up to Him. Also, keep watch for the ways that He is answering your prayers in ways you may not have expected.

❈ PRAYER ❈

Father God, let me be still and wait upon
Your timing for all my prayers. I know
You have heard them because You say You
have. Slow me down, and let my heart's
desires be Your will in my life. Amen.

❈ HEART ACTION ❈

Call upon the name of the Lord for your every need. Be patient and know that He is Lord of all. Practice patience in daily situations so you can also be patient as you wait upon God for the deep, profound life experiences.

GATHER TOGETHER

A tea party is such a wonderful way to nurture relationships with your women friends. Invite them for a Saturday morning teatime brunch. Or have tea and watch old movies or work on a project together. Get a group of your friends together for a spa day...have the staff serve tea (they usually do anyway), or take along some of your special cups and saucers and use those. What a way to enjoy a manicure or a pedicure! Be creative with your tea party... think about what you like and how you like to express yourself. Then send out those invitations. You'll be so glad you did!

There is a great deal of poetry and fine sentiment in a chest of tea.

EMERSON

FOR YOUR TABLE—A
CLEAR WINNER

Teatime is the occasion to enjoy your most beautiful cups, saucers, plates, and platters as well as your treasured china or silver tea service. But if you don't happen to own a matched set, don't let that deprive you of the pleasures of tea. Begin with what you have, borrow what you can, and give out notice among your friends and family about what you would like in the future. In the meantime, invest in a simple white ceramic pot, a creamer and sugar bowl, and an inexpensive set of white or clear glass dishes from a discount or department store. You'll need pieces to serve at least six. The beauty of this simple set is its versatility— you can transform your tea table simply by changing the linens or employing one of several creative decorating tricks. As you acquire more expensive items, the basic pieces will still supplement your tea things beautifully. There'll always be a place on any tea table for crystal-clear or pure white beauty.

Pray in Your Own Words

*Be bold and strong! Banish fear and
doubt! For remember, the Lord your
God is with you wherever you go.*

—Joshua 1:9 TLB

When you pray to God, tell Him what you want. If you do not have enough money, if you are in a tough strait, state the case—be specific in what you need. Speak in plain language; God needs no great oratories. Express your desires in the words you would normally use. They will be your best words. Name persons, name things, and take straight aim at the reason for your supplications.

One Friday night in Texas, I came down with severe fever and chills. I had to go to bed immediately when we came back to our guest suite, which was provided by our wonderful hostess in her large Texas ranch home. We usually stay in a hotel, but this particular weekend we were provided these wonderful accommodations. We had been at church all day setting up for our Saturday organizational seminar.

I was excited as always to share with women who were coming to hear how to be better wives, mothers, homemakers, and women of God.

But I was so sick! I knew that something had to change if I were going to be able to do a three-hour seminar before 500 women the next day. As I lay down on a feathery-soft bed, I immediately fell asleep until past suppertime. About ten p.m. Bob came to bed. He woke me up to see how I was doing. I awoke with a drenching sweat, high fever, and shaking chills. Bob gave me a Tylenol and water. He held me in his big strong arms and prayed, "Lord, we come before You pleading that You would make Emilie well, and that You would give her an eight-hour window tomorrow so she can teach this group of women who have anxiously waited for this day. We thank You for hearing and answering our prayers. In Jesus' name we pray, amen."

Saturday morning I woke up like nothing had ever happened, ate breakfast, and conducted my sessions with the women. God did all that we requested, and we were so thankful. On the way back to the Dallas–Fort Worth airport I began to feel bad again. Now, as I think back to the chills, fever, and sweats, I know they were the early warning signs of cancer. However, on this special weekend, the specific prayer uttered in a very simple language was heard and answered.

Father God, thanks for being a God who hears simple prayers. You have taught me that I need not be a great orator to get Your ear. You definitely give me the desires of my heart. Amen.

✳ HEART ACTION ✳

State the case. Ask. And know God is listening.

A Day Filled with Prayer

*Be joyful in hope, patient in
affliction, faithful in prayer.*

—ROMANS 12:12 NIV

Prayer is so important in our daily lives. Start each day with a prayer of thanksgiving for a new day, and end each evening with a prayer of thanksgiving for the provisions of the day. As we spend time with God, we open ourselves to His work in our hearts and in our lives. Then, as we see Him working, we will want to know Him even more. We will want our prayer life to be all that it can be. What does that mean? How should we be praying?

As meaningful as the Lord's Prayer is to Bob and me, I have also found Colossians 1:9-12 to be a powerful guide in my prayer life:

> We have not ceased to pray for you and to ask
> that you may be filled with the knowledge of His
> will in all spiritual wisdom and understanding,
> so that you will walk in a manner worthy of

the Lord, to please Him in all respects, bearing fruit in every good work and increasing in the knowledge of God; strengthened with all power, according to His glorious might, for the attaining of all steadfastness and patience; joyously giving thanks to the Father, who has qualified us to share in the inheritance of the saints in Light.

Think about how wonderful a prayer this is for you to pray for your mate and your friends!

I also encourage you to tell your friends that you are praying for them each day. If they are receptive, tell them the specifics of your prayer for them. Let me assure you that it is a real comfort to have friends praying for you, asking God to give you wisdom and understanding, to enable you to honor Him in all you do, to help you bear fruit for His kingdom, and to grant you strength, steadfastness, and patience.

Know, too, that these verses from Colossians are a good model for your prayers for other members of your family, your neighbors, and yourself. All of God's people need to know His will, honor Him in everything they do, grow in the knowledge of Him, and be steadfast as they serve Him.

❋ PRAYER ❋

*Help me, Lord, to be spiritually wise and
to pray for the people around me. Amen.*

❋ HEART ACTION ❋

Make a weekly list of family members to pray for.
Each day of the week pray for a different person.

*Let it be your business every day, in the secrecy
of the inner chamber, to meet the holy God.
You will be repaid for the trouble it may cost
you. The reward will be sure and rich.*

ANDREW MURRAY

Your Household God

*Prayer is talking with God and telling Him you
love Him, conversing with God about all the
things that are important in life, both large and
small, and being assured that He is listening.*

—C. Neil Strait

"Is it okay to pray for worldly matters?" Philippians 4:6 tells us, "In everything by prayer and supplication with thanksgiving let your requests be made known to God." Prayer is not merely for "spiritual" matters, but it's also for everyday concerns. We may take our smallest requests directly to God. He is truly our "household" God.

We all have been around eloquent people who pray with all the right words, great inflection of voice, and with enough power to not need a microphone. Their prayers are so powerful that they are intimidating, and you don't want to follow that person in prayer. We would much rather hear a prayer that is humble in nature and one that encourages us: "O Lord, I feel myself such a sinner that I can scarcely speak to You. Please help me to pray! O Lord, save my poor soul! Oh, that You would save my old friends! Lord, bless our pastor. Be pleased to give us a revival. I can say no more. Hear me for Jesus' sake! Amen."

Wow, when I hear a person pray like this, I can truly get behind that person. I know he means every single word. I don't want him to stop. His elementary style of worship through prayer truly lifts me closer to God. I am compelled to pray when he finishes his conversation through prayer.

God truly wants us to pray about the simple things of life. He is a God of the household as well as the God of the heavens. We should be specific in identifying all that we want to mention before God. We can pray for our family members, our neighbors, our church staff, our missionaries, our relatives, and our government officials. God is concerned about the smallest of our desires. Picture in your mind that God is instantly in the process of answering these household requests. A well-worded three-minute prayer is more effective than a 30-minute prayer in all of its eloquence.

❧ PRAYER ❧

Father God, let my prayers be composed
with simple and clear words. Don't let
my speech be confusing and complicated.

I want my prayers to be for those around
me and my household. Amen.

❇ HEART ACTION ❇

Pray about something you have held back on. Something simple. Or small. Or basic. God welcomes this prayer.

As long as it's hot and wet and goes down
the right way, that's all that matters.

THE DUCHESS OF YORK

Nothing but Jesus

*Ye are dead, and your life is
hid with Christ in God.*

—Colossians 3:3 KJV

We have learned in life that if we move away
from Jesus we're like the unfruitful grapevine
branch that is thrown on a pile to be destroyed. There
is a delicate balance between the branch and the
vine. In order for the branch to sprout new growth
and produce grapes, the branches need to be pruned
properly. When God is pruning us, He wants us to
grow and produce new fruit. When we go out to the
rosebushes and cut them back, we know we're not
going to like the immediate results, but come spring
we're so glad that the pruning shears removed all
those dead branches. Now there is lovely vegetation
growing where the roses have new wood to bloom.

If we are to have power in our prayers and our
Christian walk, we must be sure that we stay close
to Jesus even when the pruning shears are cutting
all the branches away in our lives. When we are in
the midst of being pruned we often ask, "Where is

Jesus when I need Him?" These are the times when we really need to cling to Him.

We are all created to worship something. Our society offers all kinds of alternatives to satisfy our worship hunger. For some people, it means they turn to a small god—like sports, wealth, fame, a job. Others choose a big God—like the Trinity: the Father, the Son, and the Holy Spirit. We must be careful in choosing whom we will serve. We must ask, "What is the object of our faith?" If it is anything or anyone other than Jesus, we must cut away all that binds us to that false god and return back to our first love—Jesus.

Satan is prowling like a lion trying to devour those who are not alert in their faith. So we need to know to whom we belong. Continue to experience the joy and the peace of fellowship with God. We should let the faith of our union with Jesus remain in us forever. Jesus is all we need!

Be on guard that Satan doesn't try to seduce you away from the Lord. Continue to abide in Jesus' holy name.

❊ PRAYER ❊

Father God, Joshua's declaration "As for me
and my house, we will serve God," is my

battle cry. Even in the midst of pruning, I
choose to serve God, my Creator. Amen.

❖ HEART ACTION ❖

Exchange your hunger for earthly things into a longing for God's heart.

Drink your tea slowly and reverently,
as if it is the axis on which the
whole earth revolves—
slowly, evenly, without rushing
toward the future.

THICH NHAT HAHN

Strike the Same Note

Seek first His kingdom and His righteousness;
and all these things will be added to you.

—Matthew 6:33

If we as believers dwell with God and God lives in us, we will desire what He desires for us. We will not deliberately ask for something that would not be pleasing to Him.

When you pray, it is important to pray for and in God's will. I know we don't always know what the Lord has for us or wills for us, and that is why it is great to bring that very concern to Him in prayer. Ask that His will be done in your life. It can be scary to pray such a thing when you know what *your* heart's desire is. Who wants to give up their control or wishes in exchange for God's? Well, hopefully *we* do…but it does take practice and prayer and a heart of submission.

Have you ever realized partway through a difficult conversation or meeting that you are not "on the same page" as your spouse, friend, or co-worker? It is like the lightbulb going on over a cartoon character's head. You suddenly understand that the two of you are seeking two different goals or outcomes. You do not share a vision for what you are striving for. It is the same in our relationship with God.

When we can so humbly approach His throne that our thoughts are open to His, we will be surprised to see how our prayers fall into line with His will for our lives. This will be true for all our petitions—sickness, death, life, children, jobs, relationships, marriage, business dealings, purchases, and so on. All supplications will come under this umbrella.

My friend, you will discover such a wonderful sense of peace and direction when you are praying for God's best for you. And when you are listening for His response and following His leading.

❧ PRAYER ❧

Father God, I don't want any of my prayers to be different than what You know is best for me. May I be humble in asking for my heart's desires—I truly don't want them if they would not be good for me. I want my prayer to be Your will. Amen.

❧ HEART ACTION ❧

Think about what "seeking His kingdom" means in your life. Get on the same page with the Lord by studying His Word and nourishing your life with His wisdom.

> *Thousands of women, at this solemn*
> *afternoon hour, were sitting behind*
> *dainty porcelain and silver fittings,*
> *with their voices tinkling pleasantly in a*
> *cascade of solicitous little questions.*

SAKI

EMILIE'S CHOCOLATE BUNDT CAKE

- ½ cup sugar
- ¾ cup water
- ¾ cup oil
- 4 eggs
- 1 small carton sour cream
- 1 package chocolate pudding, instant
- 1 box yellow cake mix
- 1 package chocolate chips
- powdered sugar

In a bowl, mix sugar, water, and oil. Mix in remaining ingredients. Pour into sprayed bundt pan. Bake at 350° F for 1 hour. Cool 1 hour and put on cake plate. Top with powdered sugar and whipped cream.

Coconut-Mint Tea

- 2 cups fresh mint leaves (from 2 large bunches)
- 8 cups double-strength fresh-brewed tea
- 1 cup coconut syrup
- 5 tablespoons fresh lemon juice

Crush mint leaves with a wooden spoon. Place mint leaves in a large teapot. Add hot tea, cup of coconut syrup, and lemon juice. Add more coconut syrup by the tablespoon and lemon juice by the teaspoon, if needed. Makes 8 servings.

❋ ❋ ❋

Ecstasy is a glass full of tea and a piece of sugar in the mouth.

ALEXANDER PUSHKIN

Become One Another

*We, who are many, are one body in Christ,
and individually members one of another.*

—ROMANS 12:5

In Scripture we often hear the terms *one spirit, one belief, one life,* and *one another.* That's when we begin to realize that God wants us to grow in oneness. Togetherness helps bond our relationship with God. Early in the book of Genesis we read, "A man shall leave his father and his mother, and shall be joined to his wife; and they shall become one flesh" (2:24).

When we join forces with others we become stronger, and it becomes difficult to weaken our positions. There is great strength in unity. This concept is at the center of why we need to be in a church that's teaching God's Word every time we meet. We need the support of others if we are to grow in Christ. We can join up with a mentor to learn the faith lessons they have gleaned from their experiences. And we can become mentors to share our stories, our failings, and our victories as Christians. This is how we strengthen our journey and build up the body of Christ.

To impress upon you the importance of oneness, today I want you to examine various scriptures from the book of Romans:

- belong to one another (12:5)
- be devoted to one another (12:10)
- honor one another (12:10)
- share with God's people who are in need (12:13)

When has someone come alongside you and offered to help you through a difficult time? It is amazing how much lighter the workload becomes when there is one other person tackling it. (Just think how much can be done when you share your load with God!) I know it isn't easy to ask for help, but give it a try. When you help someone, you feel good. When you allow someone to help you, you give them the opportunity to feel good.

❊ Prayer ❊

God, let me realize how important it is to have a support system of fellow believers who have kindred spirits. I cannot walk the journey alone—I need friends who

*will encourage me and lift me up. I am
not an island unto myself. Amen.*

❧ HEART ACTION ❧

Remember the "one another" scriptures and try
to follow them during your day. Reach out to others
and allow others to connect with and support you.

*Come, let us have some tea and continue
to talk about happy things.*

CHAIM POTOK

For God's Glory

*This sickness is not unto death, but
for the glory of God, that the Son
of God may be glorified by it.*

—JOHN 11:4

I had been under doctors' care for the previous two-and-a-half years, and my energy level was getting lower and lower, as was my weight. The travel and speaking I was doing at the time was taking its toll. I was going to a very prominent oncologist in Newport Beach, California, for a second opinion—a man who has had great success with making cancer patients well. He, too, ran his own series of tests, plus looking at all the notes from my previous doctors of the last few years. The day I was to meet him with his diagnosis for my illness, I was surrounded by family: my Bob, our son, Brad, and our daughter, Jenny. As the doctor entered into the examining room he expressed great concern about the treatment I had been receiving. He was very upset that the last nine months had been wasted with no one aggressively making decisions on my behalf.

He declared that I needed to start chemotherapy immediately. I was extremely anemic and needed two pints of blood. He also said I needed to cancel all seminars through the rest of the year if I was going to be his patient. Naturally we said, "Yes, yes, yes!" At last we had found a doctor who was proactive and wanted to make me well. After our consultation I claimed John 11:4 as my sickness verse...I wanted God to be glorified through this whole process.

What is in your life that feels like a trial or a burden? Seek to follow God's leading in the situation so that each and every day, every minute, you can faithfully give the trial over to God to be used for His glory and purposes.

❋ PRAYER ❋

Father God, thank You for medical doctors
and answered prayers. I appreciate so much
the prayer warriors all across this country
who pray for me daily. May Your Son,
Jesus, be glorified by this miracle. Amen.

❋ HEART ACTION ❋

Call a friend who is sick and let him or her know you are praying for good health. (Make the call brief.)

You should remember that though another may have more money, beauty, and brains than you, yet when it comes to the rarer spiritual values such as charity, self-sacrifice, honor, nobility of heart, you have an equal chance with everyone to be the most beloved and honored of all people.

Archibald Rutledge

God Is Bound by His Promises

*Keep watching and praying that you
may not enter into temptation; the spirit
is willing, but the flesh is weak.*

—JESUS, IN MATTHEW 26:41

God always keeps His promises. His character will not let Him fall back. In truth, all prayers offered through His Son, Jesus, are bound to be heard. God finds joy in keeping His promises.

We live in a day when all aspects of life are being undermined by dishonesty. Families have lost their retirement funds because they believed executives' promises that were made with fingers crossed behind backs. Oh, how desperate is our country for people with character! We look to our sports heroes, our political leaders, our corporate leadership, the stars of movie and television, and even our spiritual leaders, hoping they will show us how people of character live. Each time we feel comfortable that a certain personality has the answer, we are disappointed by some new revelation of broken dreams and promises.

We expect people to do what they say they are going to do. We are disappointed when a plumber, an electrician, a painter, or a co-worker can't do what they've said they are going to do. They miss the appointment or don't deliver their product on time—and here we are, waiting, and nothing happens. Even parents tell their children that such-and-such will happen on Saturday, and it doesn't happen as promised. How many children go to their rooms to cry because a promise was broken?

We are so thankful that we have one who never goes back on His promises. God the Father, Jesus the Son, and the Holy Spirit always keep Their word. If They said it, you can believe it. Let's all learn from the master of character to "just do what you say you are going to do."

❀ PRAYER ❀

Father God, thanks for being a promise keeper. You are the model for all of us. You give me great confidence in Your Word because I know You won't break a promise. If You said it, I believe it. Amen.

Make and keep a promise today—even a small one. Make this practice a discipline of your faith.

Do all the good you can, by all the means you can, in all the ways you can, in all the places you can, at all the times you can, to all the people you can, as long as ever you can.

JOHN WESLEY

The Beauty of Tea

A thing of beauty is a joy forever:
Its loveliness increases;
It will never
Pass into nothingness.

JOHN KEATS

The spirit of the tea party is, at least in part, the spirit of beauty. And I am fully convinced that we humans need beauty in order to live rich and fulfilling lives.

People grow and flourish when they are able to respond to the beauty around them and create their own forms of beauty.

And the ritual of teatime allows room for both receiving and giving loveliness.

I find that being involved with making things beautiful increases my sensitivity to the lovely things around me. Or more likely, it is the other way around. How can I possibly create a thing of beauty if I have not first experienced something beautiful?

Beauty is all around us, of course. Our world,

with all its sordid problems, still brims with breath-taking loveliness. The teatime ritual slows us down long enough to notice what is beautiful around us. In our rush to "live," we walk right by many people and things of beauty. The view outside of our own windows can offer a parade of beauty as the seasons change, and yet we often don't notice.

When I sit quietly on our patio in the morning with a cup of tea, I find I am much more acutely aware of the natural beauty around me—the swelling sunrise, the flowers blooming in their boxes by the door, the birds warming up their voices, the smell of blossoms on the breeze.

And teatime provides its own beauty as well. A traditional tea is above all a feast of loveliness, a delight to the senses.

Fingers delight in the cool smoothness of bone china, the nourishing warmth of stream rising from a cup, the contrasting textures of linen and lace, the coolness of a wafting breeze.

The nose tingles at the intoxicating mix of yeast and butter and cinnamon and roses—and tea, of course.

The ear is soothed by lovely chamber music or warm conversation or even exuberant birdsong.

Eyes revel in the dainty symmetry of tea

sandwiches painstakingly prepared and arranged, of sugar cubes piled artfully in their bowl, of violets and ferns painted delicately on the gleaming teapot.

And all this happens before my taste buds begin to experience the sweet and savory delights that have been prepared.

But let's not forget the most beautiful part of any tea—the faces of friends…the sounds of their voices…the touch of their hands…and the fragrance of friendship mingling with the lovely aroma of tea. There is deep, lasting beauty when you extend an invitation to others to gather in community.

❖ PRAYER ❖

God, let me savor the sweetness and beauty of serving others and being with friends. I'm so thankful for such joys in my life. Amen.

❖ HEART ACTION ❖

Don't hurry through your preparations the next time you are having tea. Enjoy the ritual and take in the many ways that it fills your senses.

Nowhere is the English genius of domesticity
more notably evident than in the festival of
afternoon tea. The...chink of cups and the
saucers tunes the mind to happy repose.

GEORGE GISSING

"You see, I know just how you like it."
This tea had indeed seemed to Swann, just
as it seemed to her, something precious, and
love has such a need to find some justification
for itself, some guarantee of duration, in
pleasures which without it would have no
existence and must cease with its passing.

MARCEL PROUST

Mini Tarts

- ½ cup softened butter
- 3 ounces softened cream cheese
- 1 cup all-purpose flour
- 1 batch of filling (see recipes below)

Preheat oven to 325° F. Mix butter and cream cheese until combined. Stir in flour. Roll into 24 1-inch balls. Put balls in ungreased mini muffin tins, and press evenly into the bottom and all the way up the sides of each cup. Fill each with 1 heaping teaspoon of your desired filling. Bake at 325° F for 30 minutes, until pastry is golden and filling is slightly puffed. Cool slightly in the muffin cups; then cool completely on a wire rack.

Pecan Filling
- 1 egg
- 1 tablespoon melted butter
- ¾ cup brown sugar
- ½ cup pecans

Combine ingredients in small bowl until evenly mixed.

Lemon Filling
- ¼ cup coconut
- ½ cup sugar
- ½ teaspoon shredded lemon zest
- 2 tablespoons melted butter
- 2 eggs
- 1 tablespoon lemon juice

Combine ingredients in a small bowl until evenly mixed.

❀ ❀ ❀

If man has no tea in him, he is incapable of understanding truth and beauty.

JAPANESE PROVERB

Pray for a Friend

*It is only the Lord's mercies that have
kept us from complete destruction.
Great is his faithfulness; his loving-
kindness begins afresh each day.*

—LAMENTATIONS 3:22-23 TLB

During the course of your day, pray for a friend. While you're resting, running errands, having your quiet time, or listening to music, take a moment to pray. Pray for wisdom for your friends who have children—they might need special insights as they raise those precious ones. In Colossians 1:9-12, we find a wonderful model for friendship prayer. This prayer covers…

- having spiritual wisdom and understanding
- living to honor and please the Lord
- producing every kind of good fruit
- growing as you learn to know God better and better

- being strengthened with all of God's glorious power so you will have all the endurance and patience you need.

Read the passage:

We have not stopped praying for you since we first heard about you. We ask God to give you complete knowledge of his will and to give you spiritual wisdom and understanding. Then the way you live will always honor and please the Lord, and your lives will produce every kind of good fruit. All the while, you will grow as you learn to know God better and better.

We also pray that you will be strengthened with all his glorious power so you will have all the endurance and patience you need. May you be filled with joy, always thanking the Father. He has enabled you to share in the inheritance that belongs to his people, who live in the light (Colossians 1:9-12 NLT).

What an armor of protection and growth you can give your friend with a prayer like this! Let us tell you from experience—having friends praying for us brings tremendous comfort.

❋ Prayer ❋

*Father God, I give my friendships and my
friends to You. They are wonderful gifts in
my life. Please bless them today. Amen.*

❋ Heart Action ❋

Write down in your journal a list of friends and
family members you will pray for this month. Stay
faithful to this prayer list.

*Surely every one is aware of the divine pleasures
which attend a wintry fireside; candles at
four o'clock, warm hearth rugs, tea, a fair
tea-maker, shutters closed, curtains flowing
in ample draperies to the floor, while the
wind and rain are raging audibly without.*

Thomas De Quincey

Sharing Faith

*We know that we have passed out of death
into life, because we love the brethren.*

—1 JOHN 3:14

Do you always pray for others? Probably all of us have, at one time or another, said we would pray but then forgot to do it. Not until I started working with a prayer notebook was I able to consistently remember the names of others who should be upheld in prayer. Before then someone would give me a name to pray for and I would acknowledge it, but I would often get distracted before I could pray for that person.

I realize I must pray for others because others prayed for me even before I came to know Jesus as Savior and during my lengthy bout with cancer. In Christian kindness I am led to pray for others.

Bob had a faithful Sunday school teacher who challenged him to be a godly young man. Each week she was faithful to prepare her lesson and present it to these young boys. He doesn't even remember her name, but there is one thing he will never forget—she loved those boys in her class. She prayed collectively and individually for that group.

One Easter Sunday she presented the plan of salvation as a lesson, and Bob was so touched that he gave his life to Jesus. During the Sunday-morning church service he walked down the aisle to meet the pastor at the front. He expressed his desire to know Jesus as his personal Savior. That evening Bob was baptized. To this day he credits that faithful, praying teacher for helping him make the best decision of his life.

Think of what an impression this one faithful teacher made on the lives and hearts of those she helped nurture spiritually. Who are the people in your life who are looking for a faithful teacher or example?

❖ Prayer ❖

God, what a joy to be able to pray for others. I have witnessed the power of prayer. Help me to become one who is faithful in my prayer for others. Guide me to be righteous and loving, and to be an example of Your goodness and mercy to those I am around. I want to be a woman who clears the way to faith rather than someone who is an obstacle to faith for others. Show me how to be a light. Amen.

❈ HEART ACTION ❈

Write down your testimony. Who did God use in your life to lead you to a real faith? Pray for those people today. Also, review your list of people and see how their examples can help you lead others to faith.

There are two ways of spreading light: to be the candle or the mirror that receives it.

EDITH WHARTON

THE CURATE STAND

The protocol of placing the scones on the top tier of the curate stand comes from the 1800s. During that time, when the genre of afternoon tea first became popular, modern kitchen conveniences did not exist, and a warming dome was placed over the scones. The dome would fit only on the top tier. The savories and tea sandwiches, and then the sweets, were placed on the middle and bottom tiers respectively. As the courses progressed, service would be provided to remove each tier.

- top tier: scones
- middle tier: savories and sandwiches
- bottom tier: sweets

*The privileges of the side-table included
the small prerogatives of sitting next to
the toast, and taking two cups of tea
to other people's one.*

CHARLES DICKENS

Maple-Pecan Scones

- 3 cups all-purpose flour
- 1½ tablespoons baking powder
- ¾ teaspoon salt
- 1½ sticks (¾ cup) salted butter (unsalted if desired)
- 1 cup chopped pecans
- ⅓ cup milk
- ⅔ cup pure maple syrup, plus more for brushing

Preheat oven to 350° F. Combine flour, baking powder, and salt. Cut in butter with pastry blender. Add pecans. In separate bowl, whisk together milk and syrup. Slowly pour liquid into dry ingredients while mixing, until combined. Dough should be firm. Roll out dough 1½ inches thick on floured surface. Cut scones with 3-inch round biscuit cutter. Brush tops with additional maple syrup. Place dough on greased and floured cookie sheet. Bake for 15 to 20 minutes or until golden. Makes 12.

Walk Firm and Strong

*If you have faith the size of a mustard
seed, you will say this to this mountain,
"Move from here to there," and it will move;
and nothing will be impossible to you.*

—Matthew 17:20

There is nothing too large for God. There is no force so big, no energy so spectacular that He can't control it. But if we don't believe our prayer to be effectual, then it won't be. So much mystery surrounds this word *faith*. Webster defines it as "unquestioning belief that does not require proof or evidence, unquestioning belief in God, a religion or a system of religious beliefs, anything believed, complete trust, confidence, or reliance." Hebrews 11:1 tells us, "Faith is the assurance of things hoped for, the conviction of things not seen." A few verses later, we are told that without faith, it is impossible to please God.

In my experience, having this kind of faith means we must not passively sit on the sidelines and watch others play the game of life. We must be involved. We must be loving, believing, and caring if we are to use this transforming power of the Holy Spirit to move our lives forward. We have to be active in the process. As Bob and I look back over our yesterdays, we can see how our believing in Scripture has gotten us through difficult financial, physical, mental, and spiritual times. Our enemy tries to blind us to God's truths. These fears keep us angry and bitter and leave us without peace and power. But with renewed faith, we can know we are never alone. In Christ, we can have everything we need to be victorious in the battles of life.

Sometimes our world falls apart so God can get our attention. Maybe today you need increased faith so you will be able to get through the difficult season you are in. Ask and it shall be given to you! You must ask.

❉ PRAYER ❉

Father God, my faith is increased when I think about faith. You have given me an abundance of faith, and I am thankful for that. May my faith move mountains. Amen.

❉ HEART ACTION ❉

Reflect on your faith. Share what it means to you with someone today.

If you are cold, tea will warm you;
if you are too heated, it will cool you;
if you are depressed, it will cheer you;
if you are exhausted, it will calm you.

WILLIAM GLADSTONE

I believe it is customary in good society to
take some slight refreshment at five o'clock.

OSCAR WILDE

Abide in My Love

*Just as the Father has loved Me, I have
also loved you; abide in My love.*

—Jesus, in John 15:9

If we abide in Christ, we may ask what we will, for we will ask only what the Holy Spirit moves us to ask. We won't have to wonder, but we can ask in a way that is pleasing to God. The Holy Spirit and God the Father are in full agreement about what's best for us.

As Bob and I have grown in our marriage, we have attempted to become one. Our mission statement for this is found in Genesis 2:24, which says, "A man shall leave his father and his mother, and be joined to his wife; and they shall become one flesh." Sometimes it's scary that we are so much in agreement. At times we catch ourselves finishing each other's thoughts, sentences, and even what we would like to eat for dinner. We have spent so much time together that his thoughts are my thoughts and his ways are my ways. Some people might consider this boring. We love it!

When Jesus challenges us to abide in Him, it's because He knows that the only way we can experience heavenly thoughts is to have heavenly relationships. The best way to know someone is to spend quality time together. As we spend time with our Lord, in essence we spend time with the Trinity—God the Father, God the Son, and God the Holy Spirit. It is impossible that these three should be at odds with each other. Where your prayer might be directed to one of the Trinity, they each hear and are in agreement to the answer and the proper timing of the answer. Isn't it wonderful that all three in the Trinity so love us that they are completely informed of what's best for us?

Be assured that as you approach the throne, your requests and petitions have been heard and that the Trinity will send back a response that aligns your prayer with Their will for your life.

❋ PRAYER ❋

Father God, we think we can do great things with today's communications technology, but You, the Son, and the Spirit could keep track of multiple lines of communication long before e-mail. Amen.

❧ HEART ACTION ❧

Approach the throne of the Lord today. Make your requests known.

God loves each of us
as if there were only one of us.

AUGUSTINE OF HIPPO

Abiding Provides Fruit

As the branch cannot bear fruit of itself, except it abide in the vine; no more can ye, except ye abide in me.

—John 15:4 kjv

Only as we abide in Christ can we bear fruit. We cannot say to ourselves, *What a fruitful branch I am! Look at me. The vine would not be beautiful without my presence.* Without abiding, we are no more than the dried-up branches that will be pruned, thrown on a pile, and eventually set on fire or hauled away. If our work does not come through Jesus, it counts for nothing—zero. Our fruit-producing has to go beyond our natural talent. Each of us has been called for a unique ministry. We need not copy another's ministry, because that isn't our calling. Remember, our calling is just for us, and it will not produce fruit if Christ isn't in agreement.

I have had the wonderful opportunity to speak

in almost every state of the Union as well as numerous places in Canada. Invariably I have women who come up to me and remark, "Someday I want to do just what you are doing." What a wonderful compliment that is to me. We all should think that what we do is the best career that anyone could have. I often remark that they need to be called to do God's work. If He hasn't called you to use your special gifts in this way, you will not be blessed.

Over and over again I am able to see how God enables people to reap fruit from their gifts. I want women to tell *their* story, not mine and not yours. God is preparing each of us for our unique ministry. We need to take all the roadblocks that come into our lives and make them freeways to God's truth. We can take every valley and make it a mountaintop experience.

God will teach you more in suffering than in victory. Look straight into pain, death, loss of job, a divorce, a hospital stay, and see what God is trying to teach you. Become alert to life; get in the habit of journaling the events of your life. You say you won't forget, but you will. Don't trust your memory—write down how God is using these difficult times to develop fruit in your Christian walk. Through each valley experience you are gaining information you

will use later in life. Each experience will give you an
opportunity to bear fruit for our Lord.

❀ PRAYER ❀

*Father God, I don't want to bear any fruit on
my own. Without your blessing it is nothing
but wood, hay, and stubble. Thank You
for all the blessings You send me. Amen.*

❀ HEART ACTION ❀

Start the daily or weekly habit of writing down
everything God is teaching you.

God Is a God of Love

God so loved the world, that He gave His only begotten Son, that whoever believes in Him shall not perish, but have eternal life.

—John 3:16

If we pray and we do not have love, God will ask, "Why should I hear and answer your prayers? Success will only make you think you can do it on your own." Do we really expect Him to answer our prayer when it does not include love for His community?

Are we doing that which is pleasing in God's sight? We can't expect a loving God to answer prayers from people who are unloving—after all, God is love. With today's constant threats from acts of terrorism, we find that our churches take on a whole new meaning of family. Depending upon what section of the country we live in, we readily see that our communities are very multicultural. We are a country of many sizes, shapes, colors, languages, and religions.

Are we open to what God is doing in our country as it is today? In the years following the 9/11 attacks, we find revival taking place in America. People are looking to the church for answers to large questions, and they are looking for love. For decades Americans have been looking in all the wrong places for love. Now we need to make sure that love is not only found within the walls of our churches, but within our hearts. God has given His love to us; in turn, we must give our love to the world.

❊ PRAYER ❊

Father God, where would this world be without Your love? There would be few hospitals, few orphanages, few missions, few churches, few artists, few hymns, and few musicians. The beauty would be lost. Thank You for Your love. Amen.

❊ HEART ACTION ❊

Challenge yourself to find one way to give to the world today. Volunteer. Pray for strangers. Serve others.

The Wonder of Simplicity

I say unto you, What things soever ye desire, when ye pray, believe that ye receive them, and ye shall have them.

—Jesus, in Mark 11:24 KJV

When we go to God in prayer, we go with specifics in mind. We are to have detailed desires. But prayer should not be a marketing list. Sometimes we may need to make notes to remind us not only of our desires, but also of items involving adoration, confession, thanksgiving, and supplication.

Faith is an essential quality of successful prayer. We must truly believe that God hears and will answer us. Another of the qualifications in today's verse is that we believe we receive our desires—not that we might receive, but that we *will* receive. Count your prayer requests as if you have already received them and act as if you have them. In short, there are four qualifications of prayer:

- There should be definite objects for which to plead.

- We have an earnest desire for their attainment.

- We have a firm faith in God.

- We have an expectation that we will be given what we pray for.

Many years ago, we were teaching a Bible study in our home on Sunday evenings. Most of the young adults were college students who had come home for the summer. We had a great time socializing, studying the Bible, and sharing in songs and prayers. One evening the topic was "being specific in our prayers." We couldn't just pray for an apartment, but we had to request location, amount of rent, number of square feet, number of bedrooms, color of paint on the walls, and so on. Our assignment was to report back the following week and share how and to what degree our specific prayers were answered.

The following Sunday evening as we met in the family room to share, the class members' mouths were wide open when different young people reported how God had answered their specific prayers. One girl had been looking for an apartment with seven qualifications. We were amazed when *all* qualifications were met. Well, everyone in that group started praying with specifics after that! During that summer, many of those in attendance reported how being exact gave greater meaning to their prayer time. We learned the preciousness of simplicity. God is so faithful to those who approach Him with the desires of their hearts.

Prayer

Father God, let me remember to be specific when I pray to You. I don't have to be highbrow or a great orator to have You hear me. Thanks for letting me be simple. Amen.

Heart Action

Pray specific prayers today. Lift up a specific need to the Lord this month. Journal the results.

A Home Needs Care

Older women likewise are to be reverent in their behavior, not malicious gossips... teaching what is good, so that they may encourage the young women to love their husbands, to love their children, to be sensible, pure, workers at home, kind.

—TITUS 2:3-5

One morning a very distraught lady called me. She was crying and almost hysterical. I could hardly understand what she was attempting to tell me, but after a few moments of consoling she settled down so we could have a meaningful conversation. The bottom line was that she hadn't learned one of the basic truths of being a mom. She expressed her main problem: "Emilie, I do everything you say to do in your books—and after about six weeks everything is a mess again. What am I doing wrong?" I began to chuckle silently. You see, we all have this problem with our homes. We want to fix them up and have them stay that way all of our lives. Once we begin to realize that a home is similar to the Golden Gate Bridge we will be much happier. Let me explain.

Bob and I were returning back home from Northern California when our route took us over this giant bridge. As we drove across the spans of steel, Bob told me a story about how workers no sooner get finished chipping away the rust and painting this majestic engineering feat than they have to start all over again and do the same thing. Their work is never done. As homemakers, neither is our work ever done. Until we reconcile ourselves to this fact we will always be stressed out and perhaps angry that all our work seems for naught.

We can get overwhelmed by taking care of our homes because there's always something needing to be repaired, replaced, painted, or fixed. We will be much happier when we realize that our homes are in process; our homes are where families live and grow.

❋ PRAYER ❋

Father God, let me relax in my home. I don't want to get stressed out because there is so much that continually needs to be done. Let me realize that that's life. My home is not my enemy but my friend. Thank You for giving me a home and the family that lives in it. I really appreciate how You've blessed me. You are so generous with Your gifts. Amen.

❋ HEART ACTION ❋

As you do the dishes for the third time today, be grateful that you have dishes to wash.

*The happiest moments of my life have been
the few which I have passed at home
in the bosom of my family.*

THOMAS JEFFERSON

The Inspiration of Tea

Not what we give, but what we share,
For the gift without the giver is bare;
Who gives himself with his alms feeds three,
Himself, his hungering neighbor, and me.

JAMES RUSSELL LOWELL

The very act of preparing and serving tea encourages conversation. The little spaces in time created by teatime rituals call out to be filled with conversation. Even the tea itself—warm and sweet and comforting—inspires a feeling of relaxation and trust that fosters shared confidences.

Even more important, tea nurtures friendship by inviting us to be present to one another—right now, in the moment.

So many things in our culture can be done without having to be fully aware or focused. We can go about our business without tuning in mentally and emotionally to the people around us or to the task at hand. We can drive and listen to the radio at the same time. We can eat dinner in front of the television. We can go to entertainment events or even to church and sit side by side without truly connecting with one another.

But when we offer tea to someone, we are also offering ourselves. We are saying, "I will listen to you. I will treat you with respect. I will be present for you."

Teatime supports a conversation by giving us something to do when the dialogue lags…or hits an uncomfortable snag. If we don't know what to say, we can always pick up another muffin or freshen our companion's cup or just inhale the aroma of our own cup, and thus negotiate the silences to explore deeper levels of companionship.

The relationship-enhancing properties of tea make it a wonderful vehicle for getting to know someone new, for patching up a misunderstanding, for sharing good news or supporting one another in bad times. I have seen lives change over teacups. I have seen new friendships forged and old friendships renewed.

It's not the tea, remember—it's the spirit of the tea party. And the spirit of the tea party is, above all, the spirit of true friendship.

❊ PRAYER ❊

*Lord, help me be fully present—in heart, soul,
and mind—to enjoy the sweet communion
of kindred spirits over a cup of tea. Amen.*

❊ HEART ACTION ❊

Treat your teatime companions—strangers,
friends, or family—with the same gentleness and
respect you reserve for the delicate china teacups!

*O Tea! O leaves torn from the sacred bough!
O stalk, gift born of the great gods!
What joyful region bore thee?
In what part of the sky
Is the fostering earth swollen with
your health, bringing increase?*

PIERRE DANIEL HUET

FRUITY ICED TEA

This fruity tea punch can be served with a skewer of tropical fruit or a little umbrella for added flavor and color. This recipe makes about 15 8-ounce glasses or 30 punch cups.

- 1 cup water
- 1¾ cups sugar
- 3 cups freshly brewed strong tea
- 3 cups orange juice
- 1 cup lemon juice
- 2 cups pineapple juice
- 1 quart club soda or seltzer
- ice cubes, preferably made from orange or pineapple juice

Boil the water and sugar together for 5 minutes to make a syrup. Mix the tea and juices together, then stir in the sugar syrup. Cover and chill overnight. When ready to serve, fill glass or cup half-full with concentrate, add ice, then top off glass with seltzer or club soda. If you prefer, place the entire recipe in a punch bowl, float an ice ring made from juices, and serve.

✿ ✿ ✿

[I am a] hardened and shameless tea drinker, who has for twenty years diluted his meals only with the infusion of this fascinating plant; whose kettle has scarcely time to cool; who with tea amuses the evening, with tea solaces the midnight, and with tea welcomes the morning.

SAMUEL JOHNSON

Wouldn't it be dreadful to live in a country where they didn't have tea?

NOEL COWARD

PERFECT SUGAR COOKIES

- 1 cup granulated sugar
- 1 cup powdered sugar
- 1 cup margarine or butter
- 1 cup salad oil
- 2 eggs, beaten
- 1 tablespoon vanilla
- 5¼ cups flour
- 1 teaspoon cream of tartar
- 1 teaspoon baking soda
- ½ teaspoon salt
- sugar

Cream together first 4 ingredients. Add eggs and flavoring. Mix flour, cream of tartar, soda, and salt. Add to creamed mixture. Chill. Roll out dough and create cookies with bone-shaped cookie cutter. Sprinkle with sugar. Bake on an ungreased cookie sheet at 375° F for 12 to 15 minutes, or until slightly browned. Makes 40 to 60, depending on cookie-cutter size.

About the Author

Emilie Barnes is the author of 65 books, including *The Twelve Teas® of Friendship*; *101 Ways to Clean Out the Clutter*; *Heal My Heart, Lord*; and *15 Minutes Alone with God*. She appears on over 300 radio stations as host of *Keep It Simple*. Emilie and her husband, Bob, are also the founders of More Hours in My Day™ time-management seminars.

Learn more about Emilie Barnes at
www.emiliebarnes.com

OTHER HARVEST HOUSE BOOKS
BY EMILIE BARNES

❅

Everything I Know I Learned over Tea

An Invitation to Tea

Let's Have a Tea Party!
Special Celebrations for Little Girls

A Tea to Comfort Your Soul

If Teacups Could Talk

The Twelve Teas® of Friendship

The Twelve Teas® of Inspiration

Friendship Teas to Go

More Help for Your Heart and Home
from Emilie Barnes

Simple Secrets to a Beautiful Home
Creating a Place You and Your Family Will Love

Aren't the best kinds of homemaking secrets the simple ones?

A beautiful home doesn't require too much money, too much energy, or too much time. Bestselling author and home-management expert Emilie Barnes shows you how you can easily weave beauty and happiness into the fabric of your daily life.

Simple Secrets to a Beautiful Home is an encouraging reminder that with just a touch of creativity, a splash of hospitality, and a sprinkle of welcome, you can simply enjoy, nurture, and transform your home.

To read a sample chapter of these or other Harvest House books,
go to www.harvesthousepublishers.com

Youniquely Woman
Becoming Who God Designed You to Be

Personal life coaching from three smart, spiritual women!

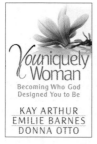

Bestselling authors and speakers Kay Arthur, Emilie Barnes, and Donna Otto have been great friends for years, and now they've come together to share the wisdom and life experience they've gained in their years of following God and being wives and mothers.

Offering straight talk on their mistakes and what they wish they'd known and put into action when they were younger, these wise, seasoned women show you how to

- live intentionally and follow the path God has for you as a woman
- develop and carry out a biblically based vision for your home, marriage, and children
- nurture your own spiritual life and the spiritual lives of your children

Kay, Emilie, and Donna have helped many women move toward all that God designed them to be—now let them help you!

To read a sample chapter of these or other Harvest House books, go to www.harvesthousepublishers.com

Good Manners for Every Occasion
How to Look Smart and Act Right

Do you ever wonder which way to pass dishes when you sit down to eat with company? Are you often confused over whose name comes first when introducing people? In this friendly guide to good graces, etiquette expert Emilie Barnes addresses these issues and more...

- proper business manners
- polite telephone protocol
- courtesy in the workplace
- entertaining without anxiety
- staying with a friend as a house guest
- graciousness while traveling

Whether you're going on a business trip, chatting at a tea party, or helping with an elegant wedding reception, *Good Manners for Every Occasion* can help you look smart and act right in every situation.

To read a sample chapter of these or other Harvest House books,
go to www.harvesthousepublishers.com

The Quick-Fix Home Organizer
Making Your Home Beautiful and Your Life Clutter Free

Only have a little time to spare? Perfect! Life just got easier and more beautiful.

Sit back and enjoy insider tips from bestselling author Emilie Barnes for beautifying and organizing your life and home while preserving your energy and encouraging your creativity. Brief, practical, and inspirational ideas will help you

- start and finish projects with success
- create a home that reflects your personal style
- find a place for the papers, clothing, or toys that pile up
- add fun and function to your rooms
- get the most out of your daily planner

Make simple changes and discover quick fixes to free up your valuable time for the more important things in life!

To read a sample chapter of these or other Harvest House books, go to www.harvesthousepublishers.com